Walking the Dartmoor Railroads

Walking the Dartmoor Railroads

Eric Hemery

DAVID & CHARLES
Newton Abbot   London   North Pomfret (Vt)

For my son Gabriel

British Library Cataloguing in Publication Data

Hemery, Eric
 Walking the Dartmoor railroads.
 1. Railroads – England – Dartmoor – Abandonment
 2. Dartmoor (England) – Description and travel –
 Guide-books
 I. Title
 385′.09423′53   DA670.D2
 ISBN 0–7153–8348–5

Photoset in Plantin by
Northern Phototypesetting Co, Bolton
and printed in Great Britain by
A. Wheaton & Co Ltd, Exeter
for David & Charles (Publishers) Limited
Brunel House, Newton Abbot, Devon

Published in the United States of America
by David & Charles Inc
North Pomfret, Vermont 05053, USA

Contents

Foreword

by Sir Peter Parker, MVO

The very name of Dartmoor conjures up in the imagination, breathtaking scenery, wild, uninhabited tors, rain and wind, sunshine and warmth: the world of the Devonian.

But, as ever, one lives and learns. Concise and to the point, factual but never boring, this book is an education even to those who already know and love the Dartmoor countryside. It is a fascinating study of industrial archaeology and social history, a guide to those who would wish to learn of the industrial life of an earlier age — primitive in some ways, but eminently practical. Especially enthralling are the descriptions of the tramroads themselves, their construction and their operation.

Naturally, as a railwayman, one loves to read of the sunny leisurely days of the Great Western Railway; to feel the peace of a summer afternoon, disturbed only by the gently passing train; to learn that the Ashburton traffic was not only passengers, but umber, malt, milk and rabbits. And let me not forget that this was Southern territory and that the Southern Railway also plays a part in this history. One can read of the formidable Meldon quarries and share, from first hand, the author's enjoyment of the company of the train crew of a quarry train.

But it is when one starts to read of the indestructible granite tramroads that one's attention is riveted by the fortitude of our forefathers. One does not read of the niceties of wagon maintenance, of permanent way renewals or of locomotive performance but of a more rugged world where, 'at the smithy, the tramway horses had their shoes examined and replaced, where necessary, before commencing the return ascent of 1400ft to the Hey Tor Quarries'.

The depth and patience of the author's research is self-evident but the result is not simply academic. The spirit of an earlier practical age lives on in this book in the wealth of detailed instruction and advice to those who want to explore the life of Dartmoor, its past and its present.

Introduction

The geographical prefix 'Dartmoor' covers the whole of the Dartmoor region, both high moorland and border-country, so that the Newton Abbot–Moretonhampstead steam-traction line is as eligible for inclusion as the Hey Tor and Zeal Tor horse-traction lines. Map 1 shows the disposition of the lines described. High Dartmoor is divided geographically into Forest and Commons; the former indicates the central area – the ancient and royal hunting ground of the sovereign, rather than dense woodland – and the latter the peripheral common land apportioned severally to the border-country parishes.

By 'following the line' is meant retracing the trackbed as it remains and where access is permissible. The term 'railroad', together with 'railway', 'railway line' and 'permanent way', is synonymous in most people's minds with a metal railroad. Rails used for steam traction, at least in Britain, have always been of iron or steel, but the Dartmoor mineral tramroads, mostly built for horse traction, have utilised three materials, iron, wood and granite, each having served its purpose satisfactorily.

The function of the Dartmoor tramroad was to enable heavy mineral and vegetable products – granite, china clay and peat – to be transported in the shortest possible time from source to canal or sea-port, and later, main railway line. (Peat is variously called by the moorland dwellers 'peat', 'blackwood', 'turf' and 'vags'. The grounds where peat is cut are the 'turf-ties' or 'peat-ties' – the terms are synonymous.) A 4-wheeled road wagon drawn by 2 heavy horses over an early nineteenth-century 'main' road could carry up to 8 tons for 20 miles (32km) at an average speed of 2–3mph (3.2–4.8kph), though such figures represent the upper limit. Delays caused by deep mud, ruts, pot-holes, fallen trees and difficult gradients were common. In striking

7

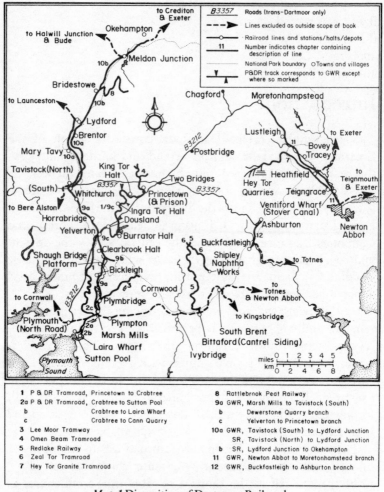

to Crediton & Exeter

Okehampton

to Halwill Junction & Bude

Meldon Junction

10b

Bridestowe

8

to Launceston

10b

Lydford

Brentor

10a

Mary Tavy

10a

Tavistock(North)

(South)

B3357

Whitchurch

to Bere Alston

9a   1/9c

Horrabridge

Yelverton

9c

Shaugh Bridge Platform

to Cornwall

B3212

Plymouth (North Road)

2a

Plympton

2b

Marsh Mills

Laira Wharf

Sutton Pool

Plymouth Sound

King Tor Halt

4

Two Bridges

Princetown (& Prison)

Ingra Tor Halt

Dousland

Burrator Halt

Clearbrook Halt

9b

Bickleigh

9a

Plymbridge

2c

Chagford

Moretonhampstead

Postbridge

Lustleigh

11

Bovey Tracey

7

Heathfield

Hey Tor Quarries

Teigngrace

Ventiford Wharf (Stover Canal)

Ashburton

12

Buckfastleigh

6 5

6

Shipley Naphtha Works

to Totnes

Cornwood

5

to Totnes & Newton Abbot

to Kingsbridge

South Brent

Bittaford (Cantrel Siding)

Ivybridge

to Exeter

to Teignmouth & Exeter

11

Newton Abbot

to Crediton & Exeter

B3212

B3357

Mary Tavy

miles 0 1 2 3 4 5

km 0 2 4 6 8

Map 1 Disposition of Dartmoor Railroads

contrast, 2 horses could haul 5 trucks along permanent way, each truck carrying up to 4 tons – a total load for 1 train of 20 tons. Mud was virtually non-existent, as were pot-holes; dying trees were removed from the trackside and gradients skilfully controlled by the use of cuttings, embankments, tunnels and inclined planes. The necessity for a good grip for the horses' hooves meant the provision of a walkway between rails; if sleepers were used, such as on the Lee Moor Tramway, a level walkway was provided by earth tightly packed between sleepers; if the tramroad were a long-distance one, for example the Plymouth & Dartmoor, rails were bolted to separate, paired granite blocks ('sets'), instead of sleepers, and small loose stones spread as a covering between rails. Lastly came the important factor of friction between vehicle wheels and road surface. Whereas, if the latter were rough and uneven, movement was impeded, the smooth and even surface of a railroad tended always to facilitate it. The tramroad speed commonly attained was 4–5mph (6.4–8kph) and, by changing horses (at specially sited stables), the entire journey on the longest tramroad (PDR, 25 miles (40.2km)) could be achieved easily in a day, with a return of the train to at least the half-way point (for the PDR, the stables at North Wharf, Clearbrook).

Thus, the planning of steam-traction railroads, when the time came, was off to a flying start; it had all virtually been done before in order to achieve the highest efficiency with horse-power. Now it was the turn of the iron horse, and, so expert was the survey in 1819–20 for the PDR that, half a century later when the GWR planned their Yelverton–Princetown branch line, they were able to adopt the earlier route with few deviations.

The lines described here have, with one exception, wholly or in part lost their permanent way; the exception is the Hey Tor granite tramroad, the line possessing a permanence quite unrivalled: being itself of granite, requiring neither sleepers nor chairs, it was bedded in the subsoil in such way as to defy its removal, short of excavation. So it is still there – except where excavated. Rural steam railway branch lines have, as we all know, received short shrift in the cause of economy. The new nationalised giant of the 1950s, British Railways, commissioned Baron Richard Beeching, PhD, later Chairman of the Board (1963–5), to report and submit recommendations on the branch lines; the result was closure of some outstandingly scenic lines (the Princetown branch a classic example), the removal of permanent way and the decay of station buildings, trackbeds and bridges. Movements are afoot today to open up some of the old tracks as hiking and cycle paths; in other cases railway preservation societies have succeeded in restoring lines to use for steam-hauled passenger trains. The latest scheme in Devon – one relevant to this book – seeks to renew the old GWR line from Plymouth through Bickleigh Vale to Yelverton. It has to date advanced sufficiently to lead the Plym Valley Railway Association to purchase the ex-Southern Railway, West Country class, 4-6-2 locomotive, *Wadebridge*.

Then there were the pipe-dreams, the schemes born of over-optimism, for in the early 1800s Dartmoor was ripe for development – or so the indefatigable developers thought. If the great peat bogs could be drained and put to the plough, and fertiliser introduced, then crops could be grown and the waste would be waste no longer – all such newly fertile areas, of course, to be served by railways. It seemed not to occur to optimists that such schemes at nearly 2,000ft (609m) in the oceanic climate of the south-west peninsula were madly impracticable. Yet if the technology of the day had been equal to them, some at least of these schemes would have been realised, for conservation had yet to raise its head, even to be born, and much of south-western Dartmoor would have changed its face materially a full century before English China Clays subjected Lee Moor to facial surgery.

Finally, a note on spellings. The names of many Dartmoor features as they appear on OS maps and in current literature are mistranscriptions. The authentic spellings (a subject dealt with in the author's *High Dartmoor: Land and People*) are used here.

1
Plymouth & Dartmoor Railway (Princetown–Crabtree Wharf)

25 miles (40.2km) Map 2

Historical digest
Thomas Tyrwhitt (1762–1833) was private secretary and personal friend of George, Prince Regent; subsequently held many important appointments; knighted 1812. Given lands on Dartmoor by Regent 1785; built residence 'Tor Royal' from local granite, also war prison at 'Prince's Town'. Following French wars, granite much in demand for buildings, bridges etc. Tyrwhitt realised commercial possibilities; submitted tramroad plan to Plymouth Chamber of Commerce 1819; royal assent 1821. Surveyor: Shillibeer; original railhead: Foggintor Quarry; afterwards depot behind Railway Inn (now 'Devil's Elbow'), Princetown, elevation 1,400ft (427m). Devon's first iron railroad; gauge $4\frac{1}{2}$ft (1.4m), chaired rails bolted to granite sets; ballast used; opened 26 September 1823 to Crabtree Wharf, Laira estuary; freight carried in both directions. John Johnson succeeded Tyrwhitt in operating quarries, tramroad; won contract for stone for Nelson's Column; quarried at Foggin Tor; despatched down tramroad in finished rounded blocks direct to Sutton Harbour for shipment. Closure details, see p102.

Following the line
From the Railway Inn depot the tramroad – Devon's first iron railroad – crossed Princetown Square, its track in later years becoming the GWR station approach and its trackbed at the station adopted by the GWR. Use the GWR track as the main guide on the Dartmoor portion of the line, noting carefully from Map 2 where deviations occur. It continued westward to Foggin Tor, where granite for a war prison at 'Prince's Town' was quarried following the French wars and a branch tramroad, known as Royal Oak Siding, was constructed to the quarry faces.

11

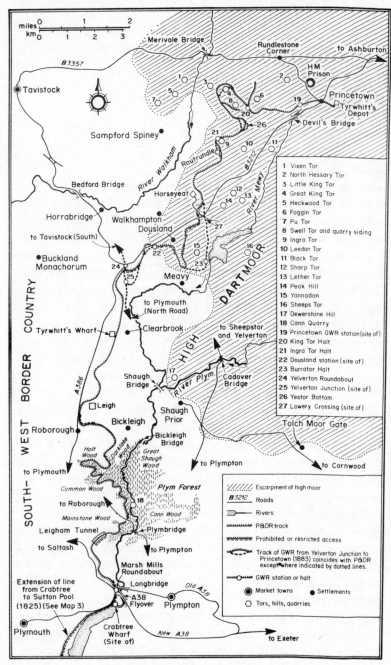

miles
km

B 3357

to Ashburton

Merivale Bridge
Rundlestone Corner
HM Prison
Tavistock
Princetown
Tyrwhitt's Depot
Sampford Spiney
Devil's Bridge
River Walkham
Routrundle
Bedford Bridge
Horseyeat
Horrabridge
Walkhampton
Dousland
to Tavistock (South)
Buckland Monachorum
Meavy
to Plymouth (North Road)
Tyrwhitt's Wharf
Clearbrook
to Sheepstor and Yelverton
Cadover Bridge
HIGH DARTMOOR
River Mewy
River Plym

1 Vixen Tor
2 North Hessary Tor
3 Little King Tor
4 Great King Tor
5 Heckwood Tor
6 Foggin Tor
7 Pu Tor
8 Swell Tor and quarry siding
9 Ingra Tor
10 Leedon Tor
11 Black Tor
12 Sharp Tor
13 Lether Tor
14 Peak Hill
15 Yannadon
16 Sheeps Tor
17 Dewerstone Hill
18 Cann Quarry
19 Princetown GWR station (site of)
20 King Tor Halt
21 Ingra Tor Halt
22 Dousland station (site of)
23 Burrator Halt
24 Yelverton Roundabout
25 Yelverton Junction (site of)
26 Yestor Bottom
27 Lowery Crossing (site of)

Shaugh Bridge
Leigh
Bickleigh
Shaugh Prior
Roborough
Bickleigh Bridge
Holt Wood
Great Shaugh Wood
to Plymouth
to Cornwood
Tolch Moor Gate
Common Wood
Plym Forest
to Plympton
to Roborough
Mainstone Wood
Cann Wood
Leigham Tunnel
Plymbridge
to Saltash
to Plympton
Marsh Mills Roundabout
Extension of line from Crabtree to Sutton Pool (1825) (See Map 3)
Longbridge
Old A38
Plymouth
A38 Flyover
Plympton
Crabtree Wharf (Site of)
New A38
to Exeter

WEST BORDER COUNTRY
SOUTH—

////// Escarpment of high moor
B 3212 Roads
Rivers
P&DR track
Prohibited or restricted access
Track of GWR from Yelverton Junction to Princetown (1883) coincides with P&DR except where indicated by dotted lines.
GWR station or halt
Market towns   Settlements
Tors, hills, quarries

Map 2 Plymouth & Dartmoor Railway (Princetown–Crabtree Wharf)

12

Here, the huge granite sections of Nelson's Column began their journey. The siding is now a rush-filled, sunken track, clearly marked near the workings by granite sets drilled to receive the chair bolts. Sets are visible (with occasional gaps) throughout to the Laira estuary, though chairs and rails are now scarce. So expertly was the tramroad engineered that in 1877, when the GWR planned a branch line from Yelverton to Princetown, their surveyors relied almost entirely upon it, excepting minor deviations, and one major one on Yannadon (OS 'Yennadon Down'). Some sets appear *in situ* north-west of Foggin Tor, but most were moved aside for the GWR wooden sleepers – now in turn torn up. Beyond the foundations of a plate-layers' hut (left) the beautiful Walkham Valley between Little King and Vixen Tors comes into view. The GWR swings left under Great King Tor to enter a rock cutting, but the PDR continues ahead on the banked-up brink of a hillside shelf below the huge tor. On the grassy curve here are three iron chairs still firmly bolted to sets and not previously recorded. The distance between sets, not constant, is approximately 6ft (1.8m). The loud sound of a klaxon in this area warns that blasting is about to begin at Merivale Quarry higher up the Walkham Valley.

The tramroad is intersected by the GWR emerging from the lower end of the cutting and became the trackbed of a GWR siding, complete with buffer stop, for loading stone at King Tor. Next follows a siding to Swell Tor (Plate 1), where the immense stone corbels lying beside the track were cut in 1903 for the new London Bridge; surplus to requirements, they were left behind and seem as though to be waiting for the train that will never come. Other worked stones appear as the siding nears the quarry in the very heart of the hill. Chosen blocks were moved on rail trucks to the masons' yard behind the buildings and shaped as needed, then stacked at the tramroad siding and crane-hoisted on to waiting trucks. From here on a clear day one may see the opposing promontories of Staddon Heights (left) and Mount Edgcumbe (right) above Plymouth Sound, between which the cargo schooners sailed for London with the Swell Tor stone 140 years ago. The wild splendour of the Walkham Valley, topped by

13

Plate 1 Swell Tor Quarry. Centre vertical is the tramroad trackbed; centre horizontal is the Plymouth & Dartmoor/Great Western siding.

many fine tors, provides a marked contrast in the westerly view, which extends far into Cornwall.

From the junction of the Swell Tor siding with the main line, the tramroad descends to Yestor Brook – here an S-bend deviation is provided by a GWR cutting – and crosses an arch-bridge. Ingra Tor follows, where a large quarry worked in the mid-nineteenth century and where relics remain of the later GWR halt. The line passes Routrundle Farm on the very edge of Dartmoor and enters the border-country above Horseyeat Farm. Continue to follow the GWR as far as the A386 road, from where the tramroad will be seen bending to the right through the (private) fields of Peakhill Farm, aligned with the remaining abutments of the PDR bridge over Peakhill Lane. A boundary wall then accompanies it (where it has been ploughed over) to the A386 at Yannadon Cross, where it enters the Dousland

14

Plantation gate opposite. It then crosses the private drive of 'The Fold' within the plantation as a banked-up level, where owner Jim Curtis has discovered numerous pieces of broken chairs and fish-plates, and emerges from the trees at Dousland electricity sub-station. It then follows Iron Mine Lane (west), where several partly buried chairs and fish-plates are visible. From here, the horse-train drivers would have seen few dwellings; now a rash of modern roofs lies between the tramroad and the distant view towards Alston Moor and Cornwall's Gunnislake, Kit Hill and Bodmin Moor. They could see also their down-line continuing beyond Meavy village to Clearbrook and the yet distant Plymouth Sound.

Approaching the old iron mine (left), the tramroad branches right from the lane and enters a private garden. Below the entrance gate is an iron rail 10ft 2½in (3.1m) long, one of a series made later to replace some of the original, shorter rails. Beyond the garden, the line coincides with the asphalted eastern portion of the lane, where modern houses stand. Beyond the lane-end gate the line executes a hairpin bend (one far too acute for steam locomotion) and rejoins the GWR, this arriving by a more graduated curve from Burrator on the east side of Yannadon. The track is next seen beyond the site of Dousland Station, where it bends south-west and runs through a field parallel with the road, the GWR and the (dry) Devonport leat. Below a transport depot it makes a compensating bend towards Yelverton, recrosses leat and road and runs through another field into Lake Lane. The track may be regained on Yelverton Green beyond Westella Garage, where it appears as a low grassed-over causeway from which a siding of granite rail-sets curved to a wharf where the shops now stand. Beyond Yelverton Roundabout, sets border the road to St Paul's Church. Continuation is clear between leat and Plymouth road, with a gradual divergence from the latter. It recrosses the leat and reaches the only remaining iron rail *in situ* on the border-country stretch of the line, another of the longer, second series. Near some large private houses here is the first surviving milestone (13); the stones, cylindrical with an inclined face bearing the

Plate 2 The two railroads in Yestor Bottom. The Plymouth & Dartmoor (between walls) negotiates an acute curve and crosses Yestor Brook on an arch-bridge (far right), while the Great Western enters a cutting (left). Fur Tor (Walkham) is top right

Plate 3 The Plymouth & Dartmoor Railway on Yelverton Green. A pre-1914 picture, showing milestone 14 which vanished during the inter-war years (*The Francis Frith Collection*)

incised figure, indicate the mileage to Sutton Pool. Beyond the houses, the tramroad appears as a wide lane between field walls (Plate 4), some sets having been removed for building the stile at each end. The pleasant hamlet of Clearbrook appears below, and beyond it are the western Dartmoor heights from Great Mis Tor to Shiel (OS 'Shell') Top.

There follows the final stretch of open country across the east flank of Roborough Down, where milestone 12, its face weathered, stands on the lower edge of Yelverton golf course. Just beyond it is 'North Wharf' (to which point granite sets are numerous), where a grand breakfast was served to 1,000 people on PDR opening day, accommodated mostly in a marquee erected for the occasion; the old building, high above Clearbrook and now used by the Golf Club, is still known as 'Tyrwhitt's Wharf'. Here, horses were changed, fed and stabled. Beyond the road climbing from Clearbrook to the A386, the line, now well below the road on a southward curve, is embanked. Beneath an oak tree here are milestone 11 and a short siding. Beyond this the line is embanked on the lower side, this whole stretch of heathland providing green and pleasant walking.

The tramroad now reaches the foot of the Dartmoor border-country and the enclosed lands begin, the hedges here being marked as 'Jump' on the PDR plan. The trackbed approaches the lane to Bickleigh from Roborough Down just below the bridge carrying the lane over the Plymouth leat. Passing through a gateway below Combepark bungalows, it follows the lower hedge of a private field before entering the gardens of bungalows nos 6 and 7. Emerging at the south end of 7 beside a field gateway, it crosses the Bickleigh lane and enters the fields of Leigh Farm, where it is seen as a shallow sunken way, its former passage through hedges shown by walled-up sections. Mr Michael Eggins of Leigh must be approached for permission to follow it, as it remains on his property until within a few hundred yards of Roborough village. It passes along the upper boundary of the farm's home field, where sets have been ploughed up and many incorporated in the hedge. Near a conspicuous oak tree here, but overgrown by brambles, is milestone 10. Leaving the

Plate 4 The Plymouth & Dartmoor Railway – granite sets near Clearbrook. Rail-chair spike-holes are visible in the sets (a small stick indicates one on the right)

home field, it enters a narrow strip-field bordered by the noisy A386 road, where its slightly raised line can be seen from the wooden roadside fence opposite the South West Gas installation. It then passes to the actual grass verge of the road at the 'Bickleigh Cross' road sign, from where it crosses the Roborough village–Bickleigh road near the Women's Institute hall and enters the private garden of 'Mera Char'. The tramroad is now fringing the environs of the great city of Plymouth, yet by its serpentine course effectively evades almost all modern developments and follows delightful woodland ways on the west Plym valley side.

Curving eastward from 'Mera Char', the line crosses two lanes branching from the Bickleigh road and approaches the first as a well-defined causeway, with a fine view towards Dewerstone Hill

18

and Shiel Top. East of the second lane (Blackaven Hill) it runs between fields and is embanked for a short way, more sets appearing near milestone 9. From the bend opposite Bickleigh village it passes through an ancient lane to Darklake, then through a wider farm lane with numerous sets into Darklake Wood, where it is highly embanked above a steep drop to the Plym Valley. Milestone 8 is here, its figure much weathered. There now follows the remarkable series of horseshoe bends where the line winds through several combes excavated by rapid streams on the west valley side. Approaching West Wood, the line is blocked by undergrowth and a wall; follow it on the fringe of the adjoining field. Entering West Wood, it runs along a hillside shelf where numerous sets and a rock cutting are seen. The scenic horseshoe bend in the combe of Holt Wood lies below the suburb of Glen Holt; near it is milestone 7. The next combe carries a stream to the River Plym in Common Wood. The line passes milestone 6 and Common Wood Cottage to run below the smallholding of 'Foresters', where a short stretch crosses the owner's land as far as the gate into Plymbridge Woods (National Trust). Here milestone 5 is missing from its vulnerable site on a southward bend; it is marked on the 1904 revision of the 1885 OS 6in map, and its disappearance is probably due to the passage of forestry vehicles during World War I when teams of horses hauled huge lumber-wagons around these bends.

Reaching the combe of Colwill Wood, the line is embanked above a picturesque stream falling steeply from the grounds of Wrigley's factory. Signs abound in Colwill Wood of the intense quarrying activity of a century ago. As the tramroad makes its nearest approach to the valley, Cann Viaduct can be seen – formerly carrying the GWR Marsh Mills–Yelverton line; adjoining the viaduct is the once busy Cann Quarry, which 150 years ago produced a high-quality blue slatestone. A canal (unfinished) was cut by landowner the Earl of Morley for the transport of the stone by barges to the Laira estuary, but was superseded by a branch of the PDR built in 1829; both features follow the river's left bank and are visible from the line in Colwill Wood. There also comes a view beyond steep wooded slopes of the Royal Marines' (42 Commando) Establishment at Bickleigh backed by the lofty line of Dartmoor's Shaugh Moor; this is, indeed, the most dramatic scenery on any part of the lowland line. Beyond the quarries the track is intersected by Plymbridge Road, where Tyrwhitt's bridge abutments still stand. Then follows a pleasant stretch in Mainstone Wood, where flowers abound in spring; milestone 4 is here, its symbol very indistinct. High embankment is followed by deep cutting, and sufficient sets (some slate) remain to guide the walker past branch paths, into the narrow Estover–Plymbridge road below Leigham.

A walk of 100yd (91m) along the road brings into view the fine granite portal of Leigham Tunnel, the second railway tunnel to be built in Britain. Leigham is 620yd (567m) long, $9\frac{1}{2}$ft (2.9m) high, $8\frac{1}{2}$ft (2.6m) wide and 109ft (33m) below ground at its greatest depth. In 1940 it was adapted for use as an air-raid shelter. Open trapdoors in the asbestos ceiling reveal the skilfully arched roof of border slate, and as the long, almost straight tube descends to its 109ft (33m), two large airshafts appear, equipped with iron ladders, though their openings are now blocked. The Mainstone sewer, installed over twenty years ago and protected by a concrete casing, runs the length of the tunnel. The concrete floor unfortunately conceals all signs of the tramroad, but an unlined length of walling, unceiled, shows clearly the high standard of the Georgian workmanship. Leigham Tunnel is now owned by the City of Plymouth, the city engineer being willing to put interested readers in touch with the lessee of the tunnel.

Below the granite portal at the lower end of the tunnel are some overgrown sets; mud and brambles make walking laborious here and milestone 3 is seen above the Landmark Filling Station in Forder Valley Road where a tremendous noise of traffic can be heard. The steep left bank, over 20ft (6m) high, is buttressed against any fall of rock or earth on to the line; this next crosses an asphalt path ascending from Leigham Mill, which is now converted to cottages – though the millstream remains. The tramroad then reaches the higher portion of Wilburt Road, but its continuation is fenced off to prevent illegal tipping in the succeeding cutting. A gap exists at the higher end of the fence

20

beyond which several sets, removed from the trackbed, are piled alongside; the line shortly becomes impassable, but can be traced visually from the main road as it borders the upper edge of a field to approach the lower (modern) loop of Wilburt Road. Crossing the modern loop road, the tramroad at once disappears into another wilderness at the higher edge of the Tecalemit factory car park where, however, it was well defined as a high embankment before clearance of the site in 1948 for the construction of the factory. Reaching the level beyond the factory site, the tramroad curved south towards the estuary below the old defensive forts of Efford and Laira, intersecting the Plymouth–Plympton road at a level crossing where it was joined by the branch line from Cann Quarry. It then passed before the Rising Sun Inn and reached Crabtree Wharf at the point of nearest approach by the deep water channel.

And that is the end of the story for the twentieth-century traveller from Princetown to Crabtree on Sir Thomas Tyrwhitt's Plymouth & Dartmoor Railway. Rails were removed from many stretches of the line in 1916 to be melted down for munitions manufacture, and industrial and roadway developments between Wilburt Road and the site of Crabtree Wharf have removed all traces of the trackbed. Of the two taverns that enjoyed the patronage of the horse-train drivers on reaching the estuary, the Crabtree Inn was demolished in 1974 to make way for the dual carriageway approaching the large Marsh Mills Roundabout, and the Rising Sun Inn, only 100yd (91m) from the site of the wharf, is now unromantically renamed the Roundabout Inn. The granite trains crossed the Crabtree plain to the wharf where ships came in to load only at high tide. It was for this reason that the tramroad was later extended to reach the quayside at Sutton Pool where no such restriction applied and from where milestone distances were calculated.

2
PDR Extensions and Branches

1¾ miles (2.8km)   Maps 3,4,5,6

Historical digest
Working limitations of Crabtree tidal wharf restricted PDR
operating; extension constructed beside Laira estuary to deep-
water quay at Sutton Harbour; certified completed by Devon
Assize Court (Exeter) December 1825. Dartmoor granite and
Cann slatestone then transferred from tramroad trucks to ships
of considerable burden. Government advanced PDR Co £18,000
to include branch lines to Laira Wharf and Cattedown Quarries;
thus, Cattedown limestone added to carriage of stone from
Dartmoor and Cann – three distinct rock-types. China clay from
Lee Moor (*c*1834) constituted fourth mineral; previously pack-
train-transported from Lee Moor to Plympton and transferred to
trucks on short PDR branch; latter sold to SDR 1847, its
function soon to be absorbed by LMT.

Large conurbation such as Plymouth detrimental to
preservation of disused inner-city railroad, yet substantial
lengths of Sutton Harbour line trackbed still traceable. Busy
harbour opens into deep waters of Plymouth Sound; inevitable
choice by John Johnson as terminal port, hence 'Johnson's
Quay'; site of wharf now occupied by Brixham & Torbay Fish
Ltd. Adjoining yard of Amey Roadstone Corporation good
viewpoint for quay; manager kindly permits (requested) entry.
Granite coping on quay wall comes as no surprise at waterside
terminal of PDR.

Following the line
Start at the Amey Roadstone Corporation yard. To reach this,
branch right from the eastbound Exeter Street, where until 1982
stood a public house named The Burton Boys, into Sutton Road.
The continuation of this road is Commercial Road and at their

22

junction appears the sign 'Lockyer Quay' on a wall, right. Opposite Lockyer Quay is a wide gateway leading to the works of Messrs Johnson & Baxter Ltd, heating engineers. The gate once controlled a level crossing, where the LSWR's Sutton Harbour line crossed Sutton Road and ran the length of Lockyer Quay and Bayley Wharf, beyond. The LSWR was eventually absorbed by the GWR, whose emblem still appears in a panel on the gate. Many people remember the siding in use, which ran to the extreme end of Bayley Wharf. A cobbled way, partly asphalted, is seen inside the gateway, diverging from the GWR trackbed and making for a modern, concrete roadside wall, right. This is the trackbed of the PDR, here pointing directly towards Johnson's Quay. Inside the gate, the premises of Johnson & Baxter show every appearance of having originated as a railside warehouse and the open space before it reveals more of the asphalted cobbled way. Here the PDR and GWR merge and at the east end of the yard the trackbed passes through a permanently closed gate. Call at Johnson & Baxter's office, left, where the managing director is pleased to allow visitors to see the yard and walk to the gate.

To view the tramroad beyond the gate, go to the railway bridge in Cattedown Road, where it is easy to park a car. Look down from the west parapet of the bridge; the trackbed appears below approaching Johnson & Baxter's east gate. The view from the opposite parapet, however, brings a surprise: there is empty trackbed no longer, but motor vehicles speeding over a modern road surface to the next overline bridge in Elliot Road. Now follow Mainstone Avenue and turn right into Laira Bridge Road; park at a safe distance from the bridge and set out on foot to follow the Laira Wharf branch and the continuing main line towards Laira Junction.

Branch line to Laira Wharf (Cattewater)
Maps 3, 4
The branch leaves the main line below the blue footbridge beside Embankment Road (it is labelled 'Marples Ridgway'). To see its approach to Laira Wharf, walk down Embankment Lane, over a

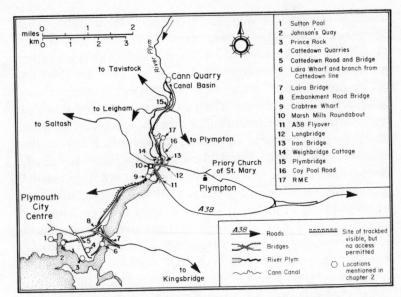

Map 3 Extension of P&DR from Crabtree to Laira Wharf and Sutton Pool, and branch line to Cann Quarry

1	Sutton Pool
2	Johnson's Quay
3	Prince Rock
4	Cattedown Quarries
5	Cattedown Road and Bridge
6	Laira Wharf and branch from Cattedown line
7	Laira Bridge
8	Embankment Road Bridge
9	Crabtree Wharf
10	Marsh Mills Roundabout
11	A38 Flyover
12	Longbridge
13	Iron Bridge
14	Weighbridge Cottage
15	Plymbridge
16	Coy Pool Road
17	RME

Map 4 P&DR track: Laira-side to Sutton Pool, 1820

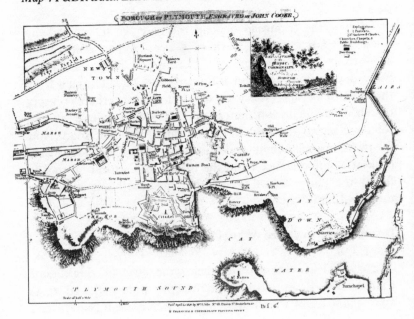

level crossing on the still used BR branch to Prince Rock and Cattewater oil terminals and pass through a wide opening beneath Laira Bridge. On the south side of the bridge a steep rocky bank rises, right, and riverside buildings and a wharf with bollards appear, left. Behind the bank are the yard and motor works of Messrs Turnbull, while the buildings (at Laira Wharf) are the 'house, stables and store thereon' owned in 1862 by the Lee Moor Porcelain Clay Company and leased by them on 27 November of that year to Rebecca Martin. From then on, Laira Wharf was known as 'Martin's Wharf'. Study the ground on nearing the wharf, which is now the property of Davies & Cann and enclosed by a wall and locked gate; between the wall and the BR line, notice vestiges of a cobbled way curving towards the wharf, and in one or two places the tips of old PDR chairs and bolts visible in the road surface. This piece of line was more or less intact as recently as 1956 and is illustrated in H. G. Kendall's *Plymouth & Dartmoor Railway*. A bird's-eye view of Martin's Wharf and the sparse remains of the line may be seen from the south (downstream) parapet of Laira Bridge. Laira Wharf (as it was known in PDR days) and the branch lines were later adopted by the Lee Moor Tramroad builders as their track and terminus at Martin's Wharf.

Main-line extension to Sutton Harbour
Maps 3,4,5
A car may next be parked near Lanhydrock Road Bridge. Walk southward along Embankment Road and turn into Maddocks Yard, another depot of Amey Roadstone Corporation. The office is on the right inside the entrance. Here ask to view the railway embankment carrying the BR Cattewater branch which bounds the yard. The embankment sides are mostly overgrown, but a bare stony patch appears in one place; this marks the site of the PDR underline crossing where the bridge opening was in-filled recently. The rear of Amey's yard is bounded by the BR main line, parallel with which runs a wide stony terrace – site of the PDR trackbed. To see traces of the line on the further, south side of the embankment, continue walking down Embankment Road

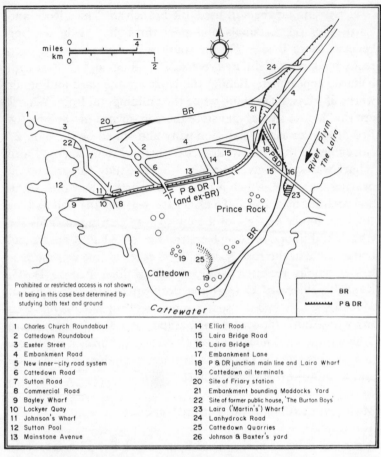

miles	0, 1/4
km	0, 1/2

Prohibited or restricted access is not shown, it being in this case best determined by studying both text and ground

——— BR
ᴗᴗᴗᴗᴗ P & DR

1 Charles Church Roundabout
2 Cattedown Roundabout
3 Exeter Street
4 Embankment Road
5 New inner–city road system
6 Cattedown Road
7 Sutton Road
8 Commercial Road
9 Bayley Wharf
10 Lockyer Quay
11 Johnson's Wharf
12 Sutton Pool
13 Mainstone Avenue
14 Elliot Road
15 Laira Bridge Road
16 Laira Bridge
17 Embankment Lane
18 P & DR junction main line and Laira Wharf
19 Cattedown oil terminals
20 Site of Friary station
21 Embankment bounding Maddocks Yard
22 Site of former public house, 'The Burton Boys'
23 Laira ('Martin's') Wharf
24 Lanhydrock Road
25 Cattedown Quarries
26 Johnson & Baxter's yard

Map 5 P&DR track-bed in 1981 from Lanhydrock Road railway bridge to Sutton Pool and Laira Wharf (Inner-city) (*Plymouth City Engineer's Dept.*)

for 80yd (73m) and turn right into Stanlake Terrace, which is parallel with the embankment's south side. Cross Stanlake Place, proceed beyond the last house (right) and step up the bank on to the PDR/LMT trackbed; beside it is another, wider trackbed, that of the former SR line (built in 1891) to their terminus at Friary. Now return to Stanlake Place and take the first right-turn, which rises above the level of the track. Emerge at Embankment Road railway bridge and view the section of line now described. Cross the road and mount the blue footbridge to view the site of the junction of the Laira Wharf line (left) and the PDR main line (ahead) under Laira Bridge Road (road-bridge), where the trackbed is now occupied by the new road system (Map 5). In the opposite, north-east direction, the PDR to Crabtree is now untraceable beyond Maddocks Yard.

Crabtree – Cann Quarry branch
2¼ miles (4.4km) Maps 3,6

This line, opened 22 November 1829, branched from the main trunk at Crabtree near the Rising Sun (now Roundabout) Inn and crossed the plain north-eastward towards the River Plym on the east side of the present Marsh Mills Roundabout. A car may be parked on the open ground beyond the Tecalemit factory entrance. As the PDR was adopted by the LMT builders in 1853, it cannot be certain that the iron rails remaining *in situ* are the original ones of 1829, although it is likely that they are, except where replacement became necessary through breakage or wear. At the eastern fringe of the roundabout, so a local man tells me who remembers the LMT track crossing the plain, the ground has been built up some 10–15ft (3–4.5m), and the line emerges at its original level and follows the verge of Longbridge Road for a short way along the river's west bank. A pleasing sight then meets the eye of the railroad enthusiast, for the PDR track, both rails surviving and flush with the road surface, turns across Longbridge Road and crosses the river on Iron Bridge. This structure of two spans with iron arches and a wooden floor was built in 1833 for the Cann Quarry branch and continued in use by the LMT until the last train ran in 1947. Passing Weighbridge Cottage (Map 3), the line received a sub-branch from Plympton Wharf (its life of very short duration) and followed a causeway across Coy Pool Marsh (now drained) into Coy Pool Road.

To park a car for the next, longer excursion, drive over Longbridge and (left) into Coy Pool Road, stopping where the roadway is wide enough near the Royal Marines Establishment (RME) (terminus of Coy Pool Road). The Establishment of the Logistic Regiment, Royal Marines, was preceded here by the

Royal Army Ordnance Corps, for whose depot the siding was built. The causeway approaches a locked gateway (left), where access is afforded by a tubular iron stile, and the track reappears on the right side of the road as a cut grass verge. Start walking here, noticing iron rails in places. On nearing the RME, notice the Establishment car park, left, the entrance gates ahead, and on the right the grass verge entering a miniature cutting; here, until 1981, the PDR rails remained, but they have since disappeared during construction by the Plym Valley Railway Association of a roadway to allow a transporter vehicle to deliver a steam locomotive (now undergoing restoration) where it stands on a specially relaid length of track. The cutting leads to the crossing of the PDR by the GWR branch line from Marsh Mills to the RME. Beside the latter is a belt of trees on the east valley side; it is threaded by four lines of communication, all parallel with the river and the RME siding – six lines in all; but, discounting the river which is not navigable above Longbridge and the siding terminating at the RME, we are left with the now united lines of LMT and PDR, the trackbed of the GWR Marsh Mills–Tavistock line and the 'tail' of the Cann Quarry Canal. To follow the tramroad as far as the site of Plymbridge Halt (GWR) is to keep in sight the three separate lines – GWR, canal, and PDR/LMT. The independent LMT line beyond its divergence from the PDR is described in Chapter 3.

On passing through Woodford Wood, there are seen pleasant, pastoral views across meadows and rivers to Mainstone Wood beyond, where runs the PDR main line (see p20). Emerging from Woodford Wood, the tramroad draws away from the high river bank it has followed, crosses the Plymbridge road on the level and enters Cann Wood to run along the canal towpath, in places only 50yd (45.7m) from the placid river. Sets, some of granite, some slate, appear north and south of the crossing and in places slabs of blue slatestone lie beside the track, perhaps fallen from tramroad trucks over a century ago and never recovered. As Cann Quarry is approached, the massive head of a spoil tip is seen, below which are the canal head basin and terminus of this picturesque PDR branch line. The terminating of the tramroad some way short of the quarry face is explained by Lord Morley's original plan for canal-transport of the slate; later, when the tramroad was built, the prior installation of quarry machinery made its extension to the quarry face impracticable, and it therefore ended at the canal basin. The intervening distance, having regard to space restrictions there, was presumably covered by man-hauled trucks on a narrow-gauge tramline, such as were commonly used in mines and quarries. According to a letter of 11 May 1855 from the Earl of Morley's solicitor (West Devon Record Office) to the quarry lessee, the last slate train had run over the tramroad on the Wednesday evening previous, 9 May, 'waggons & 2 horses' being mentioned as comprising the train.

3
Lee Moor Tramway

7 miles (11.2km) Map 6

Historical digest

China clay, product of decomposing granite, first used by Chinese (hence 'china' clay); Quaker pharmacist William Cookworthy of Notte Street, Plymouth, discovered deposit in Cornwall (Tregonning Hill near Helston) 1746. Used quayside kiln (on future site of PDR terminus seventy-four years later) for experiments in china manufacture; patented process 1768. Existence of Dartmoor deposits unsuspected until 1830. John Dickens, Plymouth earthenware dealer, found clay on Lee Moor (Lord Morley's land); opened first Devon pit; works sub-let 1833 to Sutherland glass-maker William Phillips; venture flourished. Phillips cut leats from moorland Plym and Torry Brook to supply clayworks; 1850, company re-formed as Lee Moor Porcelain Clay Co. Lord Morley acquired 500 shares on condition tramroad constructed for efficient transport of clay to Plympton Wharf, there transferred to PDR trucks (see p27). Line planned with two inclined planes (higher, Torrycombe, lower, Cann Wood), two wooden viaducts (Torrycombe and Plymbridge road) and 66yd (60.3m) tunnel at Truelove; Torrycombe Viaduct superseded 1878 by curve around valley head, Truelove Tunnel by deep cutting. Line joined PDR in Woodford Wood, clay trains using their rails to Laira Wharf. Opened 24 September 1858. Phillips died 1861; succeeded by son John; his business skills inadequate for growing industry. Firm bought by Cornishwoman Rebecca Martin; she and son Thomas highly successful. Village of Lee Moor arose; 1870 company produced 24,000 tons clay. Rebecca leased Laira Wharf (see p25); also built branch tramroad to Wotter claypit, used until 1900. Track between inclines relaid on sleepers for light locomotive traction; heavy-duty level crossing gates built at Whitegates. Horse trains

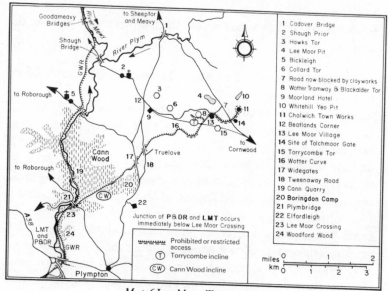

Map 6 Lee Moor Tramway

Map labels:

to Sheepton and Meavy
Goodameavy Bridges
River Meavy
River Plym
Shaugh Bridge
GWR
to Roborough
Cann Wood
Truelove
to Roborough
CW
Junction of **P&DR** and **LMT** occurs immediately below Lee Moor Crossing
to Cornwood
A38
LMT and P&DR
GWR
Plympton

1 Cadover Bridge
2 Shaugh Prior
3 Hawks Tor
4 Lee Moor Pit
5 Bickleigh
6 Collard Tor
7 Road now blocked by clayworks
8 Wotter Tramway & Blackalder Tor
9 Moorland Hotel
10 Whitehill Yeo Pit
11 Cholwich Town Works
12 Beatlands Corner
13 Lee Moor Village
14 Site of Tolchmoor Gate
15 Torrycombe Tor
16 Wotter Curve
17 Widegates
18 Tweenaway Road
19 Cann Quarry
20 **Boringdon Camp**
21 Plymbridge
22 Elfordleigh
23 Lee Moor Crossing
24 Woodford Wood

~~~~ Prohibited or restricted access
(T) Torrycombe incline
(CW) Cann Wood incline

miles 0 ___ 1 ___ 2
km 0 _ 1 _ 2 _ 3

consisted of two heavy horses and four or five deep-sided wagons, each carrying $\frac{3}{4}$ tons clay. Gauge $4\frac{1}{2}$ft (1.3m).

Following the line

The up-line is described from Martin's Wharf to Lee Moor railhead, with page numbers from Chapter 2 included to facilitate quick reference to relevant material.

Martin's Wharf–Crabtree

At Martin's Wharf, where fourteen horses were stabled, the clay schooners docked (see p25 and Maps 3,4,5). The clay trains passing by Maddocks Yard and below the BR Friary–Cattewater branch are remembered by Mr Bert Spencer of the Amey Roadstone Corporation (see p25).

Crabtree–Lee Moor Crossing

(See p27 and Map 3.) The smooth, worn look of the rails in Longbridge Road and the well-banked curve to the bridge are likely to have resulted from LMT adaptation. At the crossing of the LMT by the GWR siding to the RME a signalbox was provided, as well as a gate across the tramway up-line from the crossing.

Lee Moor Crossing – Lee Moor Terminus, Cholwich Town Pit

At the divergence of the LMT and PDR in Woodford Wood, the GWR is crossed on the level by the LMT, which moves to the extreme east side of the valley floor. Here stands the shell of a lineside building, its bricks marked MARTIN – LEE MOOR, formerly the stables for the horses used for train-hauling from the foot of the Cann Wood Incline to Martin's Wharf. Beyond it is a rotting wooden bridge that once carried the line over the canal basin, now a dangerous pit filled with dank vegetation. A passing loop and wooden viaduct spanning the Plymbridge road next follow; unfortunately, neither is now accessible, the former being overgrown and the floor of the latter, carrying the disused clay pipe, in a dangerous state of decay and blocked by barbed wire. To regain the line, therefore, return from the ruined stable to the GWR; follow it to Plymbridge Halt (site of) and take the footpath down to the Plymbridge road. Turn right, pass beneath the LMT viaduct and enter an opening in the hedge, left. Mount a steep path to reach the LMT trackbed as it emerges from the upper end of the viaduct. On the further side of the track is the private enclosure of Plymbridge Lodge. Look uphill to the Cann Wood Incline, $1\frac{1}{4}$ miles (2km) long, for which a deep and lengthy rock cutting was necessary to maintain a steady gradient (1:11); the many sets seen here are all of granite for slate would not have been equal to the strain imposed on the incline track. Openings on the lower side of the track resembling tiny branch cuttings were made to facilitate hillside dumping of excavated earth.

The wagons of the counterbalanced trains were raised and lowered by steel cables which, now lying in rusting lengths beside the track, passed over iron rollers between the rails. The laden descending train was heavier than the ascending one, even when this was carrying stores and equipment for the works, so that no power unit was required, but only a brake for each winding-drum, the control levers for which stood at track level above the

Plate 5 Lee Moor Tramway – near the foot of the Cann Wood inclined plane. Notice the cable rollers and the junction for the double track for counterbalanced trains (*Loaned by R. W. Kidner, Oakwood Press*)

underground winding-drum house at the incline head, where remaining masonry indicates its site. Interesting statistics appear in R.M.S. Hall's booklet, *Lee Moor Tramway*. Near the incline head the tramway was carried over a forest drive in Cann Wood on a wooden bridge still in sound state; signs beside the drive announce 'Forest Walk', 'Picnic Area' and 'Car Park'. The bridge carries the disused clay pipe – one's constant companion on this walk – and just below the bridge is a lineside stone bearing an inscribed 'J'. Beyond the incline, where many wooden sleepers have been prised up and lie beside the track, the tramway emerges from the wood and Dartmoor's escarpment comes into view, with Shaugh Beacon rising immediately above Shaugh Prior church. Away to the left are Bickleigh church and the Royal Marines 42 Commando barracks; further west are the large Derriford Hospital with its tall chimney, the College of St Mark and St John, and traffic following the Plymouth–Tavistock road on Roborough Down. As one follows the tramway, the Dartmoor view widens, with Dewerstone Hill, Shaden Moor, Hawks Tor, Wotter village, the high Lee Moor clay tip, Pen Beacon, Shiel Top and the huge Cholwich Town tip, above the upper terminus of the tramway, spread before one.

In this attractive undulating stretch of border-country, here threaded by the tramway, the ancient farm of Brixton Barton lies snugly in a deep little valley, left, while above, right, the fields rise gently to the large Iron Age earthwork of Boringdon Camp. The line here traverses a level, following the contour of the Brixton valley side and reaching the Plympton–Cadover Bridge road at Whitegates level crossing. The massive gate of wood and iron on the east roadside is one of two erected here in 1906, when steam locomotives were brought into use for hauling trains between the inclines. The iron casing on which the vanished gate swung still remains. Beyond the crossing the track appears inviting to follow as a narrow, grass-filled lane. A large air-vent for the clay pipe appears, several granite sets lie nearby and an embankment carried the track above a marshy bottom. This steam-traction length of the line was relaid with wooden sleepers on the original granite sets – there being no longer any need to provide a walkway for horses – thus giving the track maximum stability for locomotives. The deep cutting below Truelove Bridge (carrying the Tweenaway road to Plympton over the tramway) is in places wet and unpleasant walking; but wild flowers abound and even an apple tree has seeded since the last train passed in 1947. Mr C. Dennis of Truelove Farm well remembers the sight and sound of the locomotives steaming between his fields, heading thirty to forty laden trucks; thus the wagons of as many as ten horse-drawn trains (representing a total payload of 120 tons) were coupled and hauled between the inclines, effecting an economical use of locomotive power and necessitating almost continual daylight operation of the incline cable-drums. Production greatly increased during the 1930s and 40s and the entire system was superseded by the laying of the great 6 mile (9.6km) pipeline in 1947 from Lee Moor to the Marsh Mills drying plant, where a battery of new Buell kilns had been installed. The pipeline was laid on or beside the now redundant trackbed, the rails having been lifted. Another inevitable modernisation step, regretted by management and workers alike, was the replacement of horses at the pits by lorries and mechanical excavators. John Penderill-Church (*Lee Moor: A Brief History*) remarks that:

> ... their departure was sadly mourned. In 1920 there were about 100 horses at Lee Moor – Clydesdales and Shires, beautiful beasts, beautifully kept. These were used to pull clay wagons, to do general carting, haulage and other duties ... By 1930 they had been greatly decimated in favour of mechanized transport.

Above the Truelove cutting the track is embanked for some way and a fine medieval hedge has been breached for the tramway. Numerous granite sets lie beside the track and the walker following it into the woods on the Wotter Brook valley side receives a bird's-eye view of the mica dam, or lagoon, at Portworthy, below right, backed by the long line of Crownhill Down in the south-east. Old clay pits lie left, near the track, which rounds a horseshoe bend to cross Wotter Brook; this, the track engineered in 1878 to replace the original, unstable Wotter Viaduct is known as the 'Wotter Curve'. The line reaches the first sheds of the Lee Moor works opposite Higher Lee. Here the tramway forked, right to the Torrycombe brick and tile works, left to the Wotter Incline. A signalbox east of the junction still stands in 1983, as do two locomotive sheds nearby, at the site of Widegates level crossing where the Plympton road coming up from Coleland Bridge (Torry Brook) crossed the tramway.

Pass Higher Lee and the outlier buildings and turn left up the hill between the brick-built locomotive sheds (left) and wooden signalbox (right). For a few yards the public road ascends to Lee Moor village until this swings to the right and a works road climbs past two signs announcing, respectively, 'Reporting Centre' and 'Maximum Speed 15 MPH', and a large settling tank (left). After the latter comes another sign, 'Danger: Overhead Power Lines', and a road branching sharp right. Follow this for a short way to reach another settling tank, right; exactly opposite, the Torrycombe inclined plane rises from the left roadside, its lower portion having been supplanted by the settling tank. The incline appears as a steep grassy track, and the ridge-like obstacle ahead is the verge of the new road between the Moorland Hotel and Tolchmoor Gate; this does not yet appear on OS maps, but is shown here on Map 6. The railroad explorer using his car to reach access points on public roads can leave the vehicle on the roadside near the signalbox, walk the lower length of the incline, then drive up to the new road, park on the grass verge and ascend to the incline head to examine the remains there and the Wotter tramway.

At the incline head a trackbed approaches from the left and some ruined buildings appear at the junction ahead. The trackbed is that of the Wotter tramway, built *c*1853 to reach the pits (now exhausted) at Wotter. Its present truncated length – it is blocked by a large spoil-tip 200yd (183m) west of the junction – takes only a few minutes to walk, but it is a worthwhile diversion, for the line follows a level constructed through a considerable clitter, or rockfield, below Blackalder Tor, a bold rock-pile of the Dartmoor border-country now enclosed by oak woods and encircled by clay tips. Granite was formerly taken from the tor for building, and in 1900, when a pipeline superseded transport of clay by tramway from the Wotter pit, that end of the branch line was closed, its initial 200yd (183m) adopted for stone transport, and a loading bay (still visible) built at the quarry entrance north-west of the tor; here also was a short siding on the north side of the track. The operating of trains on the Cann Wood Incline is described on pp32–3. At the Torrycombe Incline head are various interesting remains; the look-out hut (right) was called the 'bell house', for there the look-out sounded bell signals to inform the man at the incline foot about load weights and descending trains. The latter needed to weigh 4 tons more than the ascending one – an in-balance necessitated by the steep 'nap' near the head and curve near the foot. Beyond the bell house is the castle-keep-like, brick-built, 'round house', right, where a general look-out was kept on the movement of trains approaching or leaving the incline head; almost entirely vanished are traces of the great shed that spanned the track at this point, where horses were unhitched from the down-trains arriving from railhead and cables attached for the incline descent – the procedure being in reverse, of course, for up-trains – and where in earlier days the clay trucks from Wotter were switched to the main line for the descent. Between round house and shed is the large pit that once housed the huge subterranean winding-drum, the 'drum-house', worked entirely by the gravity action of the trains and controlled by powerful brakes; the masonry of the drum-house is still in part visible. Mr H. S. Nicholson, who succeeded his father as tramway maintenance engineer in the early 1920s and lives in Lee Moor village, told me of the difficulties experienced in getting the up-train to the incline head if the counter-weight of the down-train was insufficient. Beyond the incline head the track maintains a level past Blackalder Terrace and Lee Moor Post Office (left), crosses the (Plympton) road near Lee Moor Chapel and follows the 'Sand Track' past Western Excavators Ltd at the Whitehill sheds, where it makes an abrupt north-eastward curve to approach Torry Brook's upper reach; this it formerly crossed on a stone bridge with embanked approaches, reaching the old Cornwood road at the level-crossing site just above (and south of) Tolchmoor Bridge. This stretch of line from the Whitehill sheds to the Cornwood road is now partly blocked and impassable, but the old track can be lined up in the mind's eye by standing near the crossing site and observing that the higher continuation to Cholwich Town railhead is now in use for clayworks traffic. A black shed appears on the left side of the track; this, and the wide space opposite where masses of broken, overgrown masonry lie, marks the site of the railhead of this fascinating tramway, now under the shadows of the mighty Whitehill Yeo and Cholwich Town tips.

It will be appreciated that discretion is called for in following the tramway; while public access is unimpeded between Laira and Wotter Curve – except where the walker must mount the bank from the Plymbridge road to the Cann Wood Incline and the Whitegates crossing gate – it will become obvious to anyone continuing up-line that he is entering a private industrial area, the property of English Clays Lovering Pochin & Co Ltd. The directions given here, which ECLP have kindly vetted, may be

Plate 6 Former Lee Moor Tramway level crossing, at Lee Moor, 1972. A white line is visible on the surface of the Cornwood – Cadover Bridge road (now [1983] closed to the public and submerged beneath huge clay dumps). Behind the tree are the remains of the railhead buildings. Above is Whitehill Yeo

regarded as adequate for one or two walkers, but intending party organisers should not fail to advise ECLP of their intention to lead a number of people along the route and should contact the Area Estates Surveyor, Mr G. Muskett, at Moorcroft Quarry Office, Plymstock, Plymouth, giving details of date, time and route of the proposed expedition.

4
Omen Beam Tramroad

$2\frac{1}{4}miles\,(3.6km)\,Map\,7$

Historical digest

Duchy of Cornwall granted land 1798 beside moorland Blacka
Brook to Sir Thomas Tyrwhitt for construction of mill and
bakery to supply new settlements, Prince's Town and Tor Royal.
Bakery supplied Napoleonic War prison 1809–15; following
prisoners' repatriation, tradesmen experienced hardship. Mill
('Bachelor's Hall') rented 1844 by Plymouth adventurers Jacob
Hall-Drew and Peter Adams for naphtha factory to process peat
brought from Yearlick (OS 'Greena') Ball by packhorses. In
1846 their British Patent Naphtha Company rented war
prison, built naphtha gas plant and horse-tramroad to Yearlick
Ball with branch to Omen Beam near Fice's Well. Probable
gauge $4\frac{1}{2}$ft (1.3m). Trucks of iron to withstand acidity of peat
and severe climate; stabling at prison, supplementary stable near
Fice's Well now hay-store for prison farm. Overall cost £19,000.
Ran only to prison gasworks (not to rear of Devil's Elbow Inn, as
I have seen claimed elsewhere). Ancient Blacka Brook–Peter
Tavy peat road extended to prison by French POWs; fine
clapper bridge built; entrance to prison (pre-dating gasworks)
seen at blocked, high-arch doorway in original circular wall.
Consequently, four parallel lines thread valley north of B3357 –
prison leat, tramroad, brook, peat track; first and third converge
beyond White Gate (original access to open moor pre-dating
convict farm extensions). Tramroad track spiked direct to
sleepers, with fine ballast to provide horses' walkway. No granite
sets.

Following the line

The exercise falls under two distinct headings – the admissible
north of the B3357, and the inadmissible south of it. The

39

direction and destination of the tramroad in the prison grounds, however, can be visually traced from the B3357 roadside, and I am enabled to provide a description of it here through having walked its course with the prison's chief engineering officer. From him I learnt that the tramroad had almost certainly continued in use throughout the prison's early years as a penal establishment (from 1850 onward) and that the whole building was formerly lit by naphtha gas produced from peat. Also that, early in the present century, a Crossley gas stationary engine was installed (in working order today) which ran on naphtha, and that paraffin was similarly produced from the peat.

A car may be parked at the roadside near St Michael's Church. Walk past the prison's main entrance to the next opening (right); this is the dairy yard, where a very fine stables block, dating from the building of the Napoleonic War prison, may be seen from the road; a low roof beyond this marks the site – and some original masonry – of the naphtha plant, terminus of the tramroad. (Although the dairy yard is usually open, no member of the public may enter unless escorted.) Now, continue for a short way along the road towards Rundlestone Corner (misspelt 'Rendlestone' by OS); a clear view may be seen over the wall, right, of the tramroad, embanked on a contoured shelf, leaving the gasworks (ie, the naphtha plant) and running towards a belt of trees threaded by the road ahead. A feature of interest here is a track, seen climbing from the valley floor, intersected by the tramroad and reaching a blocked roadside gateway opposite the prison quarry (left); this was the old path used by the war prisoners, and later by the 'chain-gang' convicts, from the blocked archway to their work in the quarry. From here the tramroad enters the trees and is concealed for a distance of 600yd (549m). On this stretch a streamlet from the wood was apparently allowed to flow across the track, so forming the only railroad ford in my experience. Near the north end of the wood is a larger stream, crossed by the tramroad on a massive single-opening clapper bridge. Emerging from the wood, the tramroad can be seen (but not reached) from the B3357; the walker, having viewed the quarry track, should therefore return to his car and drive to Rundlestone Corner, turn right and descend the hill to two opposing gates bearing notices. The grass verge is wide here and parking easy. Next prepare for a longer walk.

First, look over the south roadside gate, its notice reading 'Prison Property – No Admittance'. You are here actually standing on the tramroad, which follows a neatly embanked curve on leaving the wood to approach the gate. Commence your walk at the north gate, 'Gate 1' on Map 7; the notice here reads 'Prison Property' without access prohibition, and a Dartmoor National Park Authority fingerpost and yellow spot confirm the way forward through prison farm fields. The tramroad, following a low embankment, leads up the west valley side, where the open, desolate nature of the country soon becomes obvious. The walker will be on the second of the four parallel lines mentioned; the prison leat is above, the brook below and the peat track alongside it. On the crest of the opposite, east valley side is a belt of conifer trees; the hill is Omen Beam, the trees form Long Plantation and a mesh-like blanket of peat ties covers a wide expanse of hillside. Rising nobly beyond are the rocks of the Beardown Tors and ahead the domed summits of Blacka Brook Head and Black Dunghill – names somehow not inappropriate to this wide, wet and inhospitable valley. Gate 2 opens upon the second enclosure (of a strictly symmetrical field pattern). Here the brook draws closer and some interesting features appear. Just beyond Gate 3 is seen a raised track with a granite verge, parallel with the wall and descending the hill (right) to the brook. A drainage ditch has been constructed on each side of the track and is continued beyond the intersection of the peat track below. The care with which the trackbed has been laid, the existence of the drainage ditches, the directness of the whole scheme including bridges and ramps, described below, displays a refinement of plan quite unnecessary to the progress of packhorses or even horse-drawn carts. I am of the opinion, therefore, that this track was built to carry a branch tramroad from Gate 3 to the Omen Beam turf ties. This suggestion has not previously been made and, if untenable, can be laid only at my

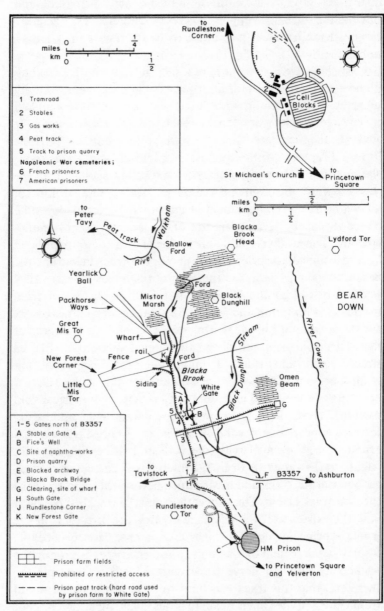

Map 7 Omen Beam Tramroad

42

door; field evidence of the laying of a metal track is so far absent, but the fact remains that the peat was brought down from the ties on the south-west slope of Omen Beam, that the trackbed is uncommonly like one built to carry a railroad, that rotovation has since destroyed the old ties, and ploughing for conifer planting has accounted for any signs that remained of a terminal wharf.

To examine the trackbed pass through Gate 3 and turn right towards the transverse wall between the peat track and the brook. The method of bringing laden trucks up the short but sharp rise from the valley floor is open to debate, but my interpretation of visible field evidence is as follows: as no winding-drum was used to haul the peat trucks up the incline – its length only 300yd (274m) – additional horses were hitched in front of the team for the haul.

The laden trucks were not pulled round a bend at the junction, as friction and gravity would have impeded this, but the entire train *continued to move upward* on the specially provided extension of raised track past the gate until the trucks could be reversed by gravity on to the main line – their movement controlled by brakes – and the normal haulage team hitched up at the front (the original rear) of the train for the gradual descent to Princetown. The 'booster' team of horses, meanwhile, would return to their stable, which I believe to have been the old building now seen at Gate 4; this was provided with a linhay, now collapsed, though the exterior door for taking in hay remains. It seems reasonable to suppose that the stable was built there, instead of at Gate 3 where the booster horses' work lay, because of the convenient proximity of fresh water, both at the brook and at the spring known as Fice's Well.

To return to the valley floor. The aperture in the brookside wall through which the Omen Beam branch passed has since been blocked. A gate was originally hung here between two large gateposts to control the movement of stock; the possibility that the peat-track gate in the branch wall was a swing gate is suggested by a worked rounded stone lying beside the tramroad, containing a deep socket in which a pivot could

Plate 7 The desolate environment of the Omen Beam Tramroad. Top left is Yearlick Ball, and Omen Beam is top right

have worked. A gateway in the riverside wall enables the walker to follow the tramroad across the brook on a massive clapper bridge of two openings, the approach at either end being a carefully constructed ramp. From here the tramroad pursues a direct eastward line to the peat ties on the south-east flank of Omen Beam at a gradient calculated to cause minimal problems. Reaching Black Dunghill Stream, the line crosses on a single opening clapper on which the track level has been maintained by a low embankment of granite blocks – something only seen on railroad bridges on Dartmoor. At the upper terminal, no turning device was necessary – the horses were merely unhitched and led to the reverse end of the train.

The northern terminus of the Yearlick Ball tramroad was at Mistor Marsh under the Ball, and in practical terms just as simple. A massive loading wharf of large granite blocks was built here, a feature previously unidentified (at least I have nowhere read of it), perhaps because it lies concealed in a slight hollow between Mistor Marsh and Blacka Brook. The height of the wharf is 5ft 4in (1.6m), the length 29½ft (9m) and the width 18ft (5.5m). Several strand-like tracks, descending over firm ground to the wharf from the peat ties on the east slope of Yearlick Ball, show where the turves were brought down by packhorses. On the opposite side of the brook are the extensive ties on Black Dunghill from where, over several centuries, turves were taken along the Peter Tavy peat track to the village of that name via Shallow Ford and Deadlake Ford (Walkham). Some points of interest, however, claim attention before the wharf is reached. Continuing northward from Gate 5, the track is embanked on the east side and carried over a gully on a sturdy little bridge. Upstream in the gully are tinners' burrows, beyond which the line enters the only true cutting on its course. The next gully is bridged by a granite conduit which has collapsed on the upstream side, causing a 'sag' in the trackbed at this point. Beyond the next gully is a built-up, branch level running eastward for 55yd (50m); this may have carried a short siding, though for what purpose is not clear. Beyond this level, however, is the trackbed of an undoubted siding, branching left and pointing directly towards New Forest Corner. As no signs of turf-cutting or loading exist, the siding may have been simply for standing spare trucks, for no loop-line is provided anywhere and the main terminus is not far ahead. Just beyond the junction lies the truly rare remnant of the tramroad – a length of iron rail *in situ*; this, the east rail of the track, is exactly 15ft (4.5m) long with a flanged base for spiking to the sleepers. On excavating the rail, I found spikes in position and fragments of sleeper wood. Despite making incisions on the west side of the trackbed, I was unable to discover another rail, and believe the track was lifted during World War I. Ground evidence suggests the gauge to have been 4½ft (1.3m).

Four more gullies, an old reave-wall (half mound, half wall) and a slightly embanked section of trackbed take the line through New Forest Gate to reach the terminal wharf. A fork in the track shown on the OS map 2½ inches to 1 mile (1:25,000) south of the reave-wall does not represent the siding described above, but the branching of the peat track (for some way up to

45

this point united with the tramroad) to approach its crossing of Blacka Brook. On arrival at the wharf, one feels the outside world to be completely excluded, but on returning along the track, the lower terminus at the prison comes into view. The granite masses of Great Mis Tor tower above this desolate scene; Blacka Brook Head and Black Dunghill, golden brown in autumn, rise north-eastward, and the Lydford and Beardown Tors dominate the background.

5
Red Lake Railway

7½ miles (12km) Map 8

Historical digest

Remote china-clay deposits at Red Lake and Left Lake Mires (Erme country) exploited after *c*1900. R. H. Worth, civil engineer, Dartmoor authority, engaged 1909 by The China Clay Corporation (1905, offices in Ivybridge) to survey railroad route to connect with GWR main line, Cantrel. Track, 3ft (0.9m) gauge spiked to wooden sleepers; inclined plane from Cantrel to RLR terminal, Cantrel Hill, elevation 900ft (274m); Red Lake railhead 1,475ft (449m). Line completed late 1910; officially opened 11 September 1911. Old Left Lake works (re-opened 1922) also served. Railway had heavy use for a decade. Machinery at Red Lake and Cantrel Incline steam-driven; transport of steam-coal priority. Workers' hostel built Red Lake. Railway carried passengers (in a tiny passenger coach – Plate 8) and general freight – never clay: this pumped to settling pits where 'micas' (unwanted solids) settled, then in water through pipeline to Cantrel 'dries'. Inspection manholes and air ducts remain along course of pipeline. Steam tractor purchased 1921, built Atkinson & Walker. Trains brought sand and fertiliser from Red Lake. By 1932 best clay exhausted; corporation liquidated 1933; track lifted by Marple & Gillott of Sheffield. GWR removed Cantrel siding and signalbox 1934; dries remained empty until 1938, then bought and adapted by H. Leon and K. Watkins as agricultural implement works; later renamed Watkins & Roseveare, now Western Machinery & Equipment Co Ltd, a division of Dutton Forshaw Group.

Following the line

The operating of the railway will become clear as the line is followed upwards from Cantrel siding to railhead. Western

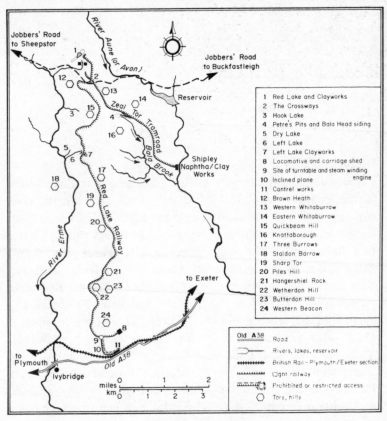

Map 8 Red Lake Railway

Legend on map:

1 Red Lake and Clayworks
2 The Crossways
3 Hook Lake
4 Petre's Pits and Bala Head siding
5 Dry Lake
6 Left Lake
7 Left Lake Clayworks
8 Locomotive and carriage shed
9 Site of turntable and steam winding engine
10 Inclined plane
11 Cantrel works
12 Brown Heath
13 Western Whitaburrow
14 Eastern Whitaburrow
15 Quickbeam Hill
16 Knattaborough
17 Three Burrows
18 Staldon Barrow
19 Sharp Tor
20 Piles Hill
21 Hangershiel Rock
22 Wetherdon Hill
23 Butterdon Hill
24 Western Beacon

Old A38   Road
Rivers, lakes, reservoir
British Rail – Plymouth/Exeter section
Light railway
Prohibited or restricted access
Tors, hills

Machinery, although modernising the site, have none the less preserved many features of the old clay-dries. The clay travelled by gravity from the Brown Heath settling tanks, suspended in water, to the works. Here its entry was controlled into fourteen large settling tanks; these have since been transformed into storage bays, although the inlets are still visible. The water was drawn off into a drainage duct and the clay transferred in blocks to the drying kiln. Three kiln doors are preserved at the west end, those at the east end having been removed. Heat was drawn through brick under-floor flues (Roman hypocaust fashion), the gases escaping into a finely built chimney stack. The dried blocks were then loaded into man-hauled trucks on a miniature tramroad – this was mounted on a raised embankment running

48

Plate 8 Red Lake Railway – a train with a passenger coach and two trucks approaches the railhead, *c*1930. Beyond, mist falls on Brown Heath (*Loaned by Mrs Stella Coles*)

the length of the building – which transported them to the storage shed; here they were taken through the large swing-up door and loaded into railway trucks on the GWR siding.

Freight of all kinds delivered by rail for the Red Lake works was unloaded at the granite siding and transferred to tramroad trucks. These were cable-hauled up the incline – originally a deep cutting but in-filled a decade ago – and at the head, run onto the turntable to be coupled behind the waiting locomotive; this, and the three passenger coaches of the line, were kept in the engine shed east of Cantrel moorgate.

The gradual ascent of the contours by the railroad was skilfully engineered by Hansford Worth and, although several cuttings and embankments were constructed, no tunnel or viaduct was necessary. Views over southern Dartmoor and the South Hams naturally become more extensive as the line ascends, and the ridges and spurs of the Erme valley rise finely ahead before the railroad walker.

Drive into Western Machinery's office car park (beside the main railway line) and call at the reception office. Ask permission to see the west-end kiln doors, the granite siding and the rising line of the inclined plane beyond the open ground west (and a little above the level) of the kilns. (It should be understood that remains inside the works are not accessible to the public and to view them would entail personal application by letter to the firm's managing director.)

From the Cantrel works, drive up the lane to the moorgate (where parking space is sufficient for only two or three cars). The hillside shelf carrying the railroad lies ahead. Pass through the pedestrian gate and turn right; notice the decaying shell of the engine shed beyond a field gate, right; this is private land – do not enter. Return along the tramroad to reach a wide space westward, observing a ruined circle of stones (a Bronze Age retaining circle) near the rough track mounting from the moorgate. Another monument of the period, a stone row, appears right, above the rail track and converging westward with it; its lower end was destroyed in constructing the railroad turntable and drum-house, which erections occupied the wide space mentioned. Several lumps of masonry remain, also the concrete bed for the steam engine which operated the incline cable. The building housing this machinery had granite gables, brick sides and a slate roof. In front of it ran a short siding which was crossed by the incline track near the turntable; the latter could accommodate only one truck at a time. The incline is, of course, directly opposite the drum-house site, and the movement of animals between the open moor and fields below was controlled by the use of a high wooden gate, hung between two piers forming ramp abutments on either side of the incline track. The gate in part remains, although now decaying. The lower portion of the incline through farm fields has been ploughed up, but its direction points slightly right of the west end of the works, to where, in fact, the granite siding remains. At the foot of the west ramp near the gate is a manhole and air-duct of the pipeline.

Return and follow the trackbed. A quarry on the north side of the line was the source of much stone for the railway sheds; directly above is Western Beacon, Dartmoor's southernmost point and 1,088ft (332m) above the distant English Channel. A diversion to the summit is worthwhile; nothing of note on the railway will be missed if the walker rejoins it some way up-line, so cutting the corner formed by the big northward curve on Cantrel Hill. There are no fewer than five burial cairns up here – a veritable sanctuary of the Bronze Age chieftains. Also prominent is a bond-stone inscribed 'H' (Harford Moor) and 'U' (Ugborough), one of a line bounding those extensive tracts of moorland. A feature connected with railway construction lies below the rocks of the tor: Western Beacon is a much weathered rock-ridge and conceals, until one almost tumbles into it, a quarry of some size, with a horse-and-cart access track leading to it from Stowford moorgate and the Ivybridge–Harford road. From this quarry, a century ago, stone was taken for the building of Bittaford and Ivybridge Viaducts to replace the fine timber structures of Brunel; in the splendid view from the tor, the former bridge is hidden by the shoulder of the hill, but the latter is clearly seen. To rejoin the railway, head nor'-nor'-west to the east slope of Wetherdon Hill (OS 'Weatherdon'); this rises west of Butterdon, the cairn-crowned hill due north of Western Beacon and part of the same ridge. Wetherdon, like most hilltops in this district, also has its cairns, but two in number and of modest size, whereas Butterdon is crowned by several very large ones. The railway is seen to curve away from Butterdon and cross the east shoulder of Wetherdon; aim for this, therefore, regaining the line as it draws away northward to pass near the prominent hillside outcrop of Hangershiel (OS 'Hangershell') Rock; from here, a fine view of the Erme valley may be seen, overlooked by the abrupt brow of Sharp Tor 3 miles (4.8km) ahead. The track continues northward with noticeable directness as it mounts the contours; it passes between two more cairn groups – right, Glascombe Ball and left, Piles Hill – before reaching the dramatic scenery of Sharp Tor and Three Burrows. In the intervening distance the line passes through several short cuttings: the soil from these was tipped on the downhill side of the track by wheeling it in barrows along the tops of the tips as they were formed; in course of time these became colonised by rabbits, and several previous writers have described them as the remains of specially constructed 'rabbit warrens' for the indulgence of sporting clay-workers. These 'warren' mounds are seen always to occur on the lower side of the track, always near a cutting, and at an inconvenient distance from either terminus; they are, indeed, no more, no less than the excavation soil-tips mentioned. Such a tip is seen as the railway approaches Piles Hill, where it also draws near to a Bronze Age stone row; this commences on Butterdon Hill and runs $1\frac{1}{4}$ miles (2km) to the Longstone, a fallen menhir on the south slope of Piles Hill. The line of the row has been continued, north of the hill and over 3,000 years later, by stones erected to mark the boundary between Ugborough and Harford Moors, this modern 'stone row' converging with the railway north of Three Burrows.

From the high col between Sharp Tor and the mountain dome of Three Burrows views are impressive, especially of the rolling ridges of southern Dartmoor and the distant shining estuary of the river that flows 650ft (198m) below Three Burrows – a name derived from the three immense prehistoric burial cairns on the summit. At the foot of the hillside near the river is the long canopy of Piles Copse, a primeval oak wood in the deep Piles Valley, protected by the dense clitter of Sharp Tor. High above this, the railway approaches a valley indenting the hillside ahead, and curves out of sight beyond Three Burrows. A further fifteen minutes' walk will bring the walker to Left Lake 'station'; here lie the ruins of the small clayworks mentioned on p47, where water from the vigorous little Left Lake was put to various industrial uses before rushing into its deep valley below the works to join the River Erme. The most impressive relic seen here is in surprisingly good condition and helpful to the walker; it is the railway bridge – a good place from which to study the old workings. Visible across the Erme Valley on the crest of the bold hill of Staldon is a remarkable Bronze Age stone row; its members, taller than the average for a Dartmoor monument of this type, suggest a procession of giants crossing the hill.

Another cutting occurs north of the clayworks, beyond which the Ugborough–Harford bond-stones converge with the railway. At this point the trackbed bends slightly westward before running north-eastward along the 1,400ft (427m) contour of Quickbeam Hill; before turning away from the valley into the track, pause and inspect the hillsides: first, 200ft (61m) below and one of a group of prehistoric hut circles, a hut has been rebuilt in medieval times. On the shoulder of the opposite, west hillside (Outer Stal Moor), is a circle of standing stones from the early Bronze Age. The row leading away northward is, at $2\frac{1}{4}$ miles (3.6km), the longest known in the world.

The walker now has two choices: either to follow the railway literally and so travel the curve of a huge bow, or to desert the line and walk along the arc of the bow, marked by the Ugborough–Harford bond-stones; the first is a gradual ascent, the second undulates via the head of Hook Lake. If the arc is chosen, no further diversion should be made after rejoining the line, for Red Lake is near ahead. The next contour loop negotiates Brown Heath, from where the lonely peatlands of the southern fen, blanket-bog source of Dartmoor's southern rivers, lie widespread beyond. While the bond-stones continue from Hook Lake to the Red Lake Valley, the railway passes through a sharply curved cutting to emerge on the north shoulder of Brown Heath; here, for 300yd (274m), it pursues a *south-easterly* course and intersects an old track approaching from the east, which descends through a sunken way to cross the Red Lake Valley on a complicated series of overgrown 'hards' across the mires to gain the north side of the valley. The track, misnamed 'Abbots' Way' on OS maps and in current literature, is the ancient Jobbers' Road, by which wild, wet and unmarked route the wool jobbers of old, local packhorse drivers who knew every detail of the way, carried their loads of wool and cloth between Buckfastleigh, Sheepstor and Tavistock. Near the intersection, on the north-west slope of Brown Heath, are the mica pits into which the clay was pumped from the Red Lake works and left to settle; another, older intersection known as 'The Crossways' occurs where the Jobbers' Road meets the Zeal Tor Tramroad

Plate 9 Red Lake Clayworks – work in progress *c*1925 (*Loaned by Mrs Stella Coles*)

and is described in Chapter 6. Another acute bend redirects the line northward, where the ruins of Red Lake works lie only $\frac{2}{3}$ mile (1km) ahead. The scenery here, on the fringe of the southern fen, is wild and desolate. When snow came early and water supply-tanks became ice-bound, steam boilers, both locomotive and stationary, had to be replenished with snow. The amount of coal burned in such conditions was prodigious. The line enters its last cutting to reach the terminus: in places here will be seen some of the only remaining sleepers *in situ*; ruins of the workmen's hostel lie left of the railhead, while on the right are those of the various workshops and the steam-engine house, where power was provided for huge pumps underwatering the workings through a shaft 120ft (36m) deep.

6
Zeal Tor Tramroad

3 miles (4.8km) Map 9

Historical digest

Notwithstanding immense deposits of rich fibrous peat on high
Dartmoor, only two railroads built to bring it down to border-
country – Zeal Tor and Rattle Brook lines. Peat at Red Lake
Mires (Erme country) unsurpassed; known to early tinners as
'blackwood'. Commercial vending not established until late
eighteenth century, when trains of heavily laden packhorses
delivered peat to market towns and mines for conversion to
charcoal. Early nineteenth-century advent of horse tramroads
revolutionised mineral transport; Red Lake peat chosen for
commercial venture of L. H. Davy and William Wilkins of
Totnes for 'cutting manufacturing and vending peat and peat
charcoal' (Duchy of Cornwall licence 11 June 1846 – Devon
Record Office) included railroad for delivering peat to treatment
works near Shipley Bridge: highly unusual construction of
wooden rails spiked to granite sets, 5ft (1.5m) gauge. Venture
failed by 1850; indenture 13 August dissolved partnership;
stipulated either Davy or Wilkins could 'carry on certain Gas
Works called the Ashburton Gas Works' while disposing of
'plant machinery tramways horses carts and stock' from Shipley
works. Tramroad remained in order; returned to partial use
1858 when another group of optimists styled 'The Brent Moor
Clay Company' purchased all stock and equipment, converted
naphtha works to clay-dries and laid branch line to clay-beds at
Bala Brook Head; remains seen today at Shipley are of clay-
dries, not earlier naphtha works. Despite increasing demand for
clay, company failed to survive owing to excess of solids in clay.
Junction for Bala Head, passing loop, workmen's shelter built
near Broad Rushes. Shelter probably existed at railhead, but
remains there not clear evidence. Stabling for horses at Middle

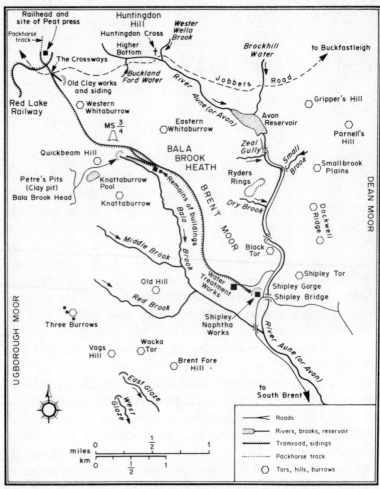

Map 9 Zeal Tor Tramroad

Brook Head (tributary of Bala Brook) in building known to moormen as 'Uncle Ab's House'. Wooden rails long since decayed, but some sets with spikes remain.

Following the line: railhead to Shipley

The $\frac{1}{4}$-mile (0.4km) stones were erected beside the track to show the up-line distance from The Crossways to Shipley; Red Lake Mires, source of the peat, was the bed of a former tarn drained by the medieval tinners and named from the profusion there of the

Plate 10 Zeal Tor Tramroad – a granite set with a spike, on Bala Brook Heath

red leaves and stems of cotton grass. Near the turf ties and beside the tramroad north of The Crossways stood a huge wooden press and loading platform; the press was screwed down upon the peat to expel the maximum moisture before loading on the tramroad trucks. Masonry and rotting timber here could possibly be relics of wharf, press and crane. Passing The Crossways, where the ancient Jobbers' Road is intersected by the tramroad, a stiff ascent begins to the shoulder of Western Whitaburrow. It is a pointer to the former importance of the old road until well into the nineteenth century that the intersection should be so named. Beside the line here are signs of a short siding and bay with built-up sides, possibly an early arrangement for collecting clay raised from a nearby shallow working. Near the tramroad at the top of the rise is the great Bronze Age cairn of Western Whitaburrow (1,580ft (481m)) named, there is evidence to suggest, by medieval travellers on the Jobbers' Road. During a survey of Brent manor bounds commissioned by Sir William Petre in

Plate 11 Zeal Tor Tramroad – the $\frac{3}{4}$ mile stone on Bala Brook Heath

1557, when the hill was recorded as 'Whyteburghe', a cruciform bond-stone (which I believe was brought from elsewhere rather than hewn here) was erected on the cairn and henceforth known as 'Petre's Cross'. Its relic remains to this day. Here the peat-cutters chose to erect a little house within the very circumference of the cairn. Sabine Baring-Gould visited Western Whitaburrow in the closing years of the century and wrote in his *Dartmoor* of the Red Lake peat-cutters:

> There being no place of shelter near, the labourers erected a house on the summit of the cairn, which measures one hundred and ninety feet in circumference, and requiring a large stone as a support for their chimney-breast, they knocked off the arms of the cross and employed the shaft for that purpose.

Springs provided water and food came up the line by train (supplemented by rabbits poached from nearby Huntingdon Warren). The viewer on Western Whitaburrow has much to see.

A good deal of the tramroad is traceable, the rabbit-breeding buries of the warren lie nearby, the immense cairn of Eastern Whitaburrow crowns the ridge a mile (1.6km) away and the great expanse of the southern fen dominates the north. It is a bracing place, leaving one in no doubt about the appetites of those early Victorian peat-cutters.

On the south-west shoulder of the Whitaburrow ridge the tramroad crosses a raised bank, or reave, the boundary mark between the Forest of Dartmoor and Commons of Brent Moor. The long descent to the Shipley works now begins; running like an arrow towards Bala Brook Heath, the line appears as a slightly sunken grass track passing in late summer through luxuriant heather. On Bala Brook Heath are numerous granite sets still retaining iron bolts, also the $\frac{1}{2}$-mile (0.8km) and $\frac{3}{4}$-mile (1.2km) stones; the former has practically lost its figure through weathering, but the latter, with a harder, more durable face, bears a clear figure. A passing loop occurs on the Heath and, near the Bala Brook valley side, a junction where the later line was laid to the Bala clay pit. Beside the loop are the remains of two buildings, one likely to have been a 'barracks' for several men, the other an outbuilding. Dimensions are: the former, $42\frac{1}{2} \times 20$ft (13×6m); and the latter 22×12ft (6.7×3.6m). Walling at gables remains to a height of 18in (457mm). The clay branch line (it became the main line after the Red Lake terminus was abandoned) runs straight to Petre's Pits, as the workings are known, where shallow pits and small overgrown tips trace a picture very different from that even at Red Lake clayworks, let alone the modern workings on Lee Moor.

The date 1877 has been given by previous writers for the adoption of the Shipley works by the clay company; this, however, conflicts with documentary evidence in the Duchy of Cornwall's London records relating to the cutting of a leat from the River Avon to Shipley for the 'Brent Moor China Clay & Mica Works Co Ltd' by a partner named William Saunders in 1858. Also, mention has not previously been made that the branch to the clay railhead was laid with iron rails; in 1953 I found some dislodged iron rails in a gully beside the clay branch (they are now overgrown and lost to view) and three clay trucks of hopper design, built by Hudson of Leeds, one of which was sinking into Bala Head Mire. A mica dam here, beneath which the brook passed through a culvert, is topped by a wide path. If Uncle Ab's House continued to provide stabling in the clayworks era – which is circumstantially likely – the horses would have been led to and from the tramroad across this dam; during the earlier period of peat-working they could cross the valley at Bala Head Ford, on which site the mica dam was later built. The walker will now appreciate the catalogue of interesting features awaiting him on Bala Brook Heath.

Between the valley and Bala Brook Heath – really the western tract of Zeal Plains – lies Broad Rushes, an aptly named expanse of common rush, around the outer limit of which the tramroad bends to run due south to Zeal Hill. Remaining parallel with the brook, it affords good views of Bala's tridental river system – the main Bala Brook, Middle Brook and Red Brook. Between tramroad and valley, on the upstream side of the Middle and Bala Brooks' confluence, is a Bronze Age farm in its private enclosing pound. Reaching the gently sloping plain of Zeal Hill, the tramroad bends south-eastward in readiness for its final descent; here again are granite sets with iron bolts. The steep descent beyond the curve poses the question: how was the movement of descending, laden trucks controlled? It is certain that no winding-drum existed; not only would local tradition relate such a feature, but I have carefully searched the ground without finding any vestige of drum-pit, base, or house; but the trucks were known to have had powerful brakes and, in addition, I believe the horses might have been unhitched on Zeal Hill and rehitched *behind* the train in order to pull back and restrain its movement. The cost of constructing a rope-controlled inclined plane was considerable and the financial story of both peat and clay undertakings at Zeal Tor makes it clear that such an installation would have been beyond the promoters' means. Indeed, the reliance on brakes as the chief mode of control on the Zeal incline has negative proof in William Crossing's *Amid Devonia's Alps*:

An old man who was employed here when the works were in full operation told me, many years ago, that he had often known the brakes, on a frosty day, refuse to act, and had more than once seen the wagons precipitated through the roof of the buildings . . .

The tramroad terminal is a steep ramp on the north verge of the settling pits. Although its incline is intersected by the new road from Shipley to the Avon Dam treatment works on Zeal Hill, it can be traced below this as a sunken way to the ramp. The culvert below the new road carried water, brought by a small capacity leat from Bala Brook, for use in the Zeal Farm fields.

It is often assumed that the tramroad carried the clay from Bala Head to Zeal Tor, but it should be made clear that, like its more modern counterpart between Cantrel and Red Lake, it was used only for transporting men and materials – excepting, perhaps, the section laid with iron rails between the Bala Brook Heath Junction and Petre's Pits, where tip-trucks were used for carrying waste. A leat, formerly cut to bring water from Bala Brook to the naphtha works, was utilised by the clay firm to convey clay, suspended in water, to their works. Here it ran into an oblong granite-lined pit, where the micas were separated from the clay; a series of circular pits, also granite-lined, lie stepwise on the hillside and were rendered confluent by small conduits; the final process took place in a larger, deeper pit (above the present car park), where the clay was cut into blocks and ejected through five huge slat-like openings in the masonry into the drying house, the site now occupied by the car park. Waste water flowed into a sediment pit below the road before returning to the river below Shipley Bridge.

Following the tramroad is straightforward rather than easy; the steady climb can be exhausting in the teeth of a strong north-west wind, for the high col between Whitaburrow and Brown Heath is excessively exposed; but, given good weather conditions, it is a rewarding expedition over open moorland, unimpeded by enclosures of any kind. Cars should be left in the Shipley Bridge car park.

7
Hey Tor Granite Tramroad

10 miles (16km) Map 10

Historical digest

Hey Tor's superb twin granite bosses visible from far out to sea – landmark of the 'high' tor. (Acknowledged Dartmoor authorities use spelling 'Hey'.) Excellence of Hey Tor granite for building recognised over two centuries ago; transportation over 10 miles (16km) by horse and wagon from quarries to Stover Canal until 1820 uncompetitively slow. George Templer (1781–1843), lessee of several quarries on Heytor Down, solved problem by building unique tramroad of granite 'rails', 3–8ft (0.9–2.4m) long, flanged on inner side, forming track of $4\frac{1}{4}$ft (1.3m) gauge. Curves – skilfully built with straight lengths; 'points' – metal cheek pieces at junctions deflecting truck wheels on to desired line; stability – stones bedded in ground, needing no rail joints. Tramroad ceremoniously opened 16 September 1820.

Compact, durable granite found over wide area of Heytor Down to brink of Houndtor Combe; five separate quarries within those limits; tramroad siding built to each; additional ancillary sidings exist – never properly mapped, now too overgrown to record. One cutting only, at top of ascent from Holwell Quarry, where

> Nineteen stout horses it was known
> From Holwell Quarry drew the stone.

Milestones erected giving distance from Ventiford to Heytor Quarry. At one small quarry, associated industry developed: John MacCarthy in 1824 manufactured 'Patent Paving Stones', paying royalty to Templer's company; relevant agreement (Devon Record Office) 9 March 1824

George Templer engages to permit the said John MacCarthy to pass over his rail road from the Haytor Quarries to his Canal at Ventiford Bridge with wagons of the same description and the same kind of wheels as are used by George Templer and not to carry a greater weight on four wheels than three Tons, the said George Templer keeping the said rail road in good repair . . .

Two relevant indentures (DRO) between Viscount Courtenay and Templer: 19 September 1825 covers passage across Lower Down, tramway 32ft (9.7m) wide, yearly rental 5 guineas; 21 January 1829 refers to 'Hay Tor Rail Road', signed and sealed by Templer with oval seal bearing dragon rampant. Finally, 18 December 1878, Surrender of Lease (DRO) signed by 'Haytor Granite Company', includes passage through Yarner Wood. Templer's business acumen fallible; in late 1820s forced to sell Stover estate, railroad, canal to Duke of Somerset. Late history of line one of disharmony, lost contracts; by 1858 tramroad no longer in regular use; sporadic use probably continued for further twenty years, then moorland turf and heather, in-country brambles and shrubs took over. Many granite sets since prised up; railroad now piecemeal with best preserved stretches on open moorland. Elsewhere, trackbed traceable except where obliterated by building and passenger railway development. Tramroad trucks open-sided, possibly converted road wagons; no known relics exist.

Following the line
The system on open moorland: It is wise to wait for favourable weather in order to begin by visiting all the upper termini, dividing the area into two walks.

Walk 1 Park a little to the south of a bend in the Bovey–Widecombe road, about midway between Saddle and Hey Tors. Walk north-eastward towards Emsworthy Rocks (a tor unnamed on published maps), itself equidistant from the two major tors. When only a short way from the road notice the magnificence of Saddle and Hey Tors. Emsworthy Rocks comprise a tor far less compact than the two giants; in reality an

63

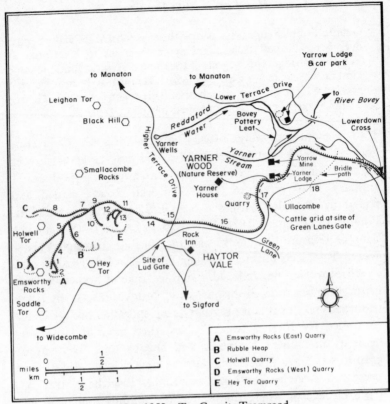

Map 10 Hey Tor Granite Tramroad

elongated, excessively weathered rock-ridge, its lower west tip reaches to the brink of Houndtor Combe. Make now for the near, east end of the ridge and take stock from the summit. Hey Tor rises on the right; left are the huge stone mounds of Rubble Heap; ahead runs the long, straight but overgrown (although not buried) line of the tramroad from a quarry below towards a conspicuous solitary tree left of Rubble Heap; this is a good guide to the junction of the line with that from the western Emsworthy Quarry, seen crossing the down. Beyond it rises another fine tor, Holwell, though less lofty than either Saddle or Hey. Here it is possible to visualise the whole of Walk 1.

Quarry A (Emsworthy East): study the triangular rail system on Map 10; ground evidence suggests that 1 was to have been extended uphill a short way, but the gradient was probably

64

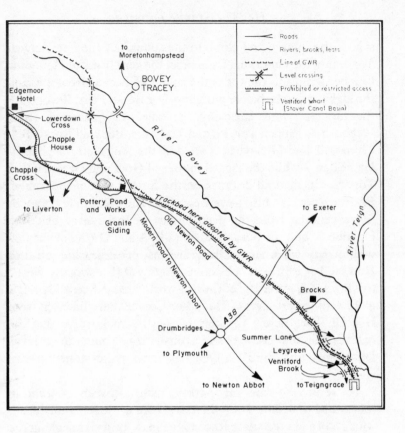

found to be prohibitive and no sets were laid. Sets are discernible in 2; at the junction of 1 and 3 is a remaining iron bolt of the switch mechanism, and a short length of line (the centre of the trident) sufficient for shunting two or three trucks. Notice that the terminus of 3 is reached through a narrow cutting. Next follow line 4 to junction 5 beside the thorn tree. Then follow line 6, from a nearby up-line junction, to *Quarry B* (Rubble Heap), where it terminates on an open plain and where much spoil and rubble from the main Heytor Quarry was tipped to avoid blocking its approaches. Return to the line and ascend to junction 7, where junction stones may be seen. From here take the scenic descent westward to *Quarry C* (Holwell), where the tramroad terminates at the foot of an immense sheer face, near the ruins of workers' cots and tool stores. Walk round the east side of the quarry and climb to the summit of the fine Holwell Tor; enjoy the panorama from here, the very brink of Houndtor Combe. Rising to the tor is the sound of Becka Brook passing through the combe before plunging over Becka Falls. Beyond are the tors and hills enclosing the vale of Widecombe (East Webburn) – Rippen Tor, Pil and Top Tors, Bonehill Rocks, Bel, Chinkwell and Honeybag Tors and the long, lofty skyline of Hameldon – while the jagged masses of Grea and Great Hound Tors rise in the mid-distance on the further side of the combe. Eastward comes a bird's-eye view of the Holwell Quarry branch-line ascending from the deep hollow of the quarry below to junction 7, and the lines to quarries B, A and D – all delineated with clarity when snow-filled. The last of these, due south of Holwell Tor is the next objective. *Quarry D* (Emsworthy West): this lies at the lower end of the Emsworthy rock-ridge and gives a more detailed prospect of Houndtor Combe than that seen from Holwell Tor. Below the summit of the rock-ridge, the line reaches a circular crane-base, its construction similar to others at Dewerstone and Ingra Tor Quarries; the junction stones at 3 are visible.

To return to the car park, choose between continuing southward to Saddle Tor (where are more workmen's cots) from where a broad green path leads to the park, or walking along the crest of the Emsworthy rock-ridge to rejoin, in reverse, the opening route of this walk. Bond-stones appear in places marking the meeting of the Ilsington and Bovey parish boundaries and are inscribed 'I' and 'B'.

Walk 2 Drive eastward along the Bovey road, turn left at Lud Gate (the road junction to Haytor Vale) into Higher Terrace Drive (leading to Manaton) and park where the tramroad crosses the road (15), or on top of the rise ahead. Follow line 14, one of the best preserved stretches of any. A deeply flanged curve occurs before junction 11, showing clearly the method of curve-construction with straight sets; a short loopline on a low embankment (12) branches near junction 11 and joins 13 at the main quarry; 13, meanwhile, is carried across a stream coursing

Plate 12 Hey Tor Granite Tramroad – a junction (of lines 12 and 13 on Map 10) near the main quarry. Notice the curve constructed with straight sets. In the distance are the twin bosses of Hey Tor

through a tinners' gert on a substantial embankment; this is now crumbling and the stream culvert partly blocked. *Quarry E* (Hey Tor): the track continues well defined as it rounds the foot of a large tip to enter the main quarry, where Heytor Ponds lie, and where a large sheer-legs crane survived the climate until well into the present century. Near the tramroad here are remains of more quarrymen's cots.

Now follow the direction of a branch line (10) from the west quarry face to junction 9; it is mostly overgrown, so make for the crest of the down and locate junction 7 on Walk 1; turn eastward here and notice the junction sets at 9. Pass through the cutting and start the gentle descent towards junction 11, where the points system is particularly well preserved. Next follow the main line down to Higher Terrace Drive at 15, beyond which it converges with and follows the Bovey road for ½ mile (0.8km). Observe the crest of the down above, left; when this is seen to decline steeply at about point 16, leave the tramroad and climb to the crest, where a wonderful in-country panorama may be seen; walk westward along the ridge of the down and notice the woodland bowl of Yarner, below right, and as Walk 2 ends, the

67

old terraced houses of Haytor Vale, left, built by George Templer during the early nineteenth century for his employees.

The in-country line

Drive down the Bovey road to the junction with Green Lane (right), where a car may be parked as an alternative to the quarry lane at 17. The tramroad is here very close to the north verge of the road, and just below the Green Lane junction a manhole cover (for underground telephone cables) marked POST OFFICE TELEPHONES, lies beside it; but the 'GPO marking post' of which Ewans writes in *The Haytor Granite Tramway and Stover Canal* has been removed; 25yd (23m) below the manhole, milestone 6 stands on the north bank, its figure weathered but still clear. Opposite the stone is the only conspicuous granite set here. Continue driving down the main road and take a concealed turning (left) into a stony lane, 17; the cattle-grid beyond the turning marks the site of Green Lane Gate, the former moorgate here. Park in the disused quarry. Walk back along the lane, noticing a gateway, left; the tramroad approaches from ahead and descends to the lane. First follow it upward to point 16 to link with the moorland sections followed; a few sets are still visible along here. Notice, opposite a bungalow named 'The Brake' on the further side of the road, that the tramroad runs between the road verge and an old watercourse; here the bank suffered an earth-slip some decades ago and sturdy trees now grow in the resulting gully. Return, following the line through the gateway; more sets are visible as it descends to a barn and cattle-yard built across it. Return to the car, drive down the Bovey road and turn (hairpin left) into the road to Yarner House (now Yarner Farm). Park outside the drive entrance opposite a modern bungalow. Mr K. E. Allerfield of Yarner Farm kindly allows walkers to enter the drive and follow the tramroad line. This, descending from the north side of the barn and cattle-yard, runs along the edge of an old sunken lane to follow the boundary fence of the Yarner drive, with which it curves to Yarner Lodge and passes through the drive gateway (between drive and tramroad in the copse is a pile of sets, and others near the Lodge).

It is well preserved in running from the Lodge into a field gateway opposite the bungalow. No traces remain in the field beyond and it is next visible (trackbed only) entering Yarner Wood at the eastern extremity of the field. Its passage is traceable, having some stretches with well-preserved sets, through the wood and beyond on Lower Down; difficulty in retracing begins as the line reaches the houses near Lowerdown Cross. The thorny subject of access raises its head – though with good reason – from the upper Yarner boundary downwards, but the fascinations of this stretch of line merit all the time given to following it.

The line in Yarner Wood
Yarner Wood has been a Nature Reserve since 1952. Enter from Lower Terrace Drive, continue past Yarrow Lodge (the reserve warden's house) and park in the reserve car park beyond. Leaflets are available here; refer to *The Woodland Walk*; cross the stream (Reddaford Water) below the park and notice the old Yarner fishponds, where frogs now breed. Proceed to post 7; notice the depth of the valley, left, of Yarner Stream, a tributary of the River Bovey rising at Yarner Wells. At post 7 the Bovey Pottery leat (from Becka Brook) flows beneath the track and the reserve workshops stand in a bay above the stream. Take the steep climb to post 4, passing the masonry remains of the engine and pumping house of the old Yarner Copper Mine (also known as Yarrow Mine). No less than 2,500 tons of copper were raised in the seven years 1858–65. Continue to the high boundary of the reserve; at a barbed-wire fence blocking the T-junction path, right, the tramroad trackbed is visible, though completely overgrown, approaching from the field hedge mentioned above. At the fence is a notice prohibiting entry to the reserve at this point. Follow the T-junction path eastward; after a slight ascent it forks; walk left, into an area of arresting scenery. The woods, beautiful at any time of the year, clothe the steep hillsides on each side of the Yarner Stream valley, where the track is seen ascending from Yarrow Lodge. Workings of the copper mine appear below, in mid-distance Yarner House overlooks the

valley and above all rides the eastern escarpment of the moor from Black Hill to Trendlebeare Down. Through this fairyland the old tramroad pursues its way, with sets numerous in places, succeeded by a perfect, 400yd (366m) length of permanent way. A sharp curve (built with straight sets) occurs, and in places dates and initials have been carved on the stones. I find '1851' interesting; the carving certainly dates from that period and, I believe, records the replacement of a broken stone by a new one. The figure '58' on another set close by may have the same significance. If so, regular use of the line in the 1850s is indicated, though it may have become intermittent by 1858. (Other writers have claimed that it ceased totally – I would suggest otherwise, in view of the above, the construction of Granite Siding at Bovey as late as 1866, a statement in *Murray's Guide* of 1865 that 'stone *is* carried down on a granite tramroad', and the circumstantial likelihood of its use by the Yarrow mining company for carrying copper ore down to Granite Siding for transfer to MSDR trucks.) On the bank above the descending track, right, and 200yd (183m) from the lower boundary gate, is milestone 5, a fine stone bearing a bold, deeply cut figure; 150yd (137m) nearer the gate is a set with the incised letters 'IC'. At the lower end of this intact length of line is the wired and padlocked gate of the reserve with, as before, a notice prohibiting passage. Return to the car park.

The line on Lower Down
Drive to Lowerdown Cross; turn right, ascend for about a mile (1.6km) to a junction with cross-tracks 18; left is the sign indicating Furzeacre and Ullacombe Cottages, two more signs (right) and a fingerpost read, respectively, 'No parking on this road', 'No unauthorised vehicles beyond this point' and 'Bridle path to the Bovey–Manaton road at Reddaford Water'. Park with discretion and follow the bridle path northward past the rear of a large house; as the path descends beside a field fence (left) two vertical stones are seen a little distance apart; neither bears an inscription, but one is carefully shaped with a rounded top, and both are likely to mark estate bounds. (Avoid walking in

70

shorts on this narrow path which is bordered on either side by gorse bushes in mutual contact to knee height.) At a clearing are two gates (point 19) where the tramroad appears (left) as a green gully under the brow of Lower Down and (right) as an overgrown path on the verge of a bracken field. (Do not, therefore, make this walk during summer months.) In descending, the line passes a set stone – possibly another bondmark – and a set removed from the trackbed. Walking improves as the line enters a copse where sets remain *in situ*; at the lower end of the copse is a tree and shrub nursery containing exotic varieties of rhododendrons and magnolia. Although no notice prohibits access, it is wise to respect this specialised use of the ground and walk circumspectly. A large private house appears ahead and the tramroad bends slightly right to reach the fence of a private orchard. Beyond, but now inaccessible, was the first crossing by the tramroad of the Bovey Pottery leat; the bridge has disappeared, however, and nothing remains to be seen. Do not mount the fence, but return up-line to the reserve gate reached in Yarner Wood. Sets continue to be visible, but rainwater has washed down silt from the steep side of the down and deposited it on the trackbed. Notice that a tramroad set does duty as a gatepost at the reserve gateway. From the shrub nursery to Lowerdown Cross is a 'no access' area; drive, therefore, to Lowerdown Cross.

Chapple area

Turn right at the Edgemoor Hotel and continue beyond a dip in Chapple Road to a bend at the end of a copse (right). Park on the verge. Granite sets are at once visible, emerging below a gate from the copse, which can be entered between gate and hedge. It is a place of delight, alive with woodland birds in the nesting season and with clearings large enough to admit plenteous sunshine; the owner, who appreciates both the historic nature of the tramroad and the interest of those wishing to follow it, is kindly willing that readers should disregard the one or two 'Private' notices they will see, in return for care and consideration in passing through the copse, which is here followed in a westward, up-line direction.

After a short distance the line is carried across a gully by an embankment beside a woodland pool; continuous sets lead to another embankment, this time across a mining gully. The gradient increases and milestone 4 appears on the right-hand bank, the figure clearly showing eighteenth-century influence; the gully, of course, corresponds with the dip in the road east of the hotel (see above). At the north end of the copse is a roadside notice reading 'To Whisselwell Farm – no parking'. Leave the copse, cross the Whisselwell turning and observe a wide flat road verge (beyond which appears the hotel); although this is the tramroad trackbed, sets are no longer visible. At Lowerdown Cross, look over a padlocked gate bounding a tiny copse, where the trackbed forms a direct line to a private garden, the owner having removed sets in order to cultivate a lawn. The house here is the lowest of those beside the Hey Tor road, the highest being near the private orchard mentioned. As the tramroad leaves the padlocked gate it crosses a deep drainage ditch on a granite culvert. Up to this point in the narrative, the tramroad has been followed from its upper termini to its emergence from the Chapple copse, where sets continue but are much grass-overgrown. At the entrance to Chapple House, several sets removed from the trackbed appear in the roadside curb and the entrance walls, beyond which the narrowed trackbed is no more than an overgrown gully. At a bend just beyond, a stream appears, right, and the road is wide enough to park a car. Here is the second crossing by the tramroad of the Bovey Pottery leat, deceptively like a natural stream. The bridge is a clapper of several granite imposts, the only one remaining of the three former bridges on the line. It is evident that the roadside wall is contemporary with the tramroad, for the wide verge between the copse and Chapple Bridge was the trackbed and the hedge built to replace the original one. At the bridge the function of the hedge was continued across its width by iron bars, the holes drilled to receive them being visible in the masonry. Beside the next bridge, carrying lane over leat, a granite set has been stood on edge, and the tramroad enters a green lane branching from the east roadside. This is signed 'Public Bridle Path', the line being embanked for some way above a drainage ditch (left). Isolated sets alternate with continuous stretches of permanent way, and the little town of Bovey Tracey is visible, quite near, with its modern housing development on the further hillside of the Bovey Valley.

Pottery area

The line emerges from the green lane east of Chapple Cross on the Brimley road (beside a terrace of Edwardian villas beginning with 'Rothesay'); crossing the road it follows another fingerposted bridle path to the Liverton road. Sets, though only just beneath the path surface, are virtually invisible; at the further end of the path, the line crosses (beside the sign 'Sharptor View') to pass behind a row of houses. Near the further end is milestone 3, leaning out of vertical. Beyond this the environment suddenly gains scenic interest: an area of open land appears (left) occupied by Pottery Pond, the original reservoir for the pottery works fed by the leat first mentioned on p69; vegetation here includes many varieties of sedge and rush attractive to water birds, trees grow along the brink, and the pond provides a pleasing oasis in an area of sprawling light-industrial development. The sluice and conduit through which water was released to the works is seen at the lower end of the pond beside the tramroad. East of the pond the trackbed is entirely obliterated by works developments, but it ran on the south side of the pottery to reach the Bovey–Newton Abbot road, crossing it just south of Pottery (railway) Bridge. From the pond, Pottery Road leads into the Newton Abbot road opposite its junction with two branch turnings (left). The second and lower is Old Newton Road; the first, however, is the immediate objective – a short, rough track. Park beside the track out of the path of lorries using it.

The final stretch of the line

The area at the end of the rough track, formerly a county council dump, is soon to be swallowed by a road-building scheme – at the obvious sacrifice of an interesting relic, the site of the tramroad's terminus after 1861 when the Moretonhampstead & South Devon Railway was built; later the GWR, the trackbed illustrated in Ewans' book is now a jungle. The tramroad entered from the north verge of Pottery Road and was carried over a gully among the trees by a short bridge with iron tramway rails – the only metals used on the entire system. From the bridge it was embanked to a raised stone platform; of this, despite general neglect, the greater part remains at the time of writing: it is Granite Siding, where the load was transferred from the tramroad train to MSDR flat trucks. The original tramroad trackbed, prior to the construction of railway and siding, continued at ground level from the gully bridge and passed beneath a modern works building, beyond which it became absorbed by the railway for $2\frac{1}{4}$ miles (3.6m) to a point just beyond Summer Lane Bridge, near Teigngrace. The combined lines may therefore now be followed as far as Heathfield Industrial Estate, where the metals of the ex-GWR line remain in place for freight use and further progress would constitute trespass. (A call at the former Heathfield passenger station is perhaps more relevant to Chapter 14, but the following motoring directions will serve for both chapters: from Bovey's Old Newton Road turn left into the A38, then first left to the station. On leaving, continue along the A38, turn into the first slip road and cross the flyover in order to return along the west-bound carriageway. The Teigngrace road is then the first turning, left.) The line of the tramroad may be viewed from the parapets of the three bridges crossing it between Heathfield and Ventiford: these, in down-line order are, the A38 bridge, one carrying a narrow lane eastward to Brocks from the Teigngrace road, and Summer Lane. The Teigngrace road is historically the continuation of Old Newton Road; Summer Lane branches abruptly left from it, reaching the railway bridge in 250yd (229m). Three minor deviations between the GWR and tramroad occur below Summer Lane Bridge, but the older line is now virtually untraceable and Ventiford becomes the final stage in following it – though its terminus at the canal wharf was unfortunately destroyed in the construction of the MSDR embankment. Just south of Leygreen, where the tramroad was crossed on the level by Leygreen Lane, the Ventiford Brook passes beneath the road to flow to the River Teign; the tramroad is likely to have crossed the brook on a simple granite bridge, before terminating at the wharf. A track runs from the road along the brook's right bank; passing beneath the railway bridge it leads to fields beyond. (No car must be parked at any point on this track, either east or west of the railway bridge. Ample roadside space exists at Leygreen, 150yd (137m) to the north.) At the junction of track and road is a private house named 'Ventiford' (formerly an inn) with, at its north end, a low-roofed annexe named 'The Forge'. This represents a well-devised conversion of the former smithy into a self-contained cottage, leaving the atmosphere of the place almost undisturbed. At the smithy, the tramroad horses had their shoes examined and replaced where necessary before commencing the return ascent of 1,400ft (427m) to Hey Tor Quarries; indeed, a smith was still shoeing here for local farmers within living memory. Two buildings aligned with the entrance gate of 'Ventiford', near the house, bear the appearance of late eighteenth-century work and are likely to have been the clay cellars and (later) stabling for the tramroad horses; temporary shelter and refreshment for canal bargees and tramroad teamsters alike was therefore available on the spot.

8
Rattlebrook Peat Railway

5¾ miles (9.2km)   Map 11

Historical digest

Large-scale nineteenth-century development of peat workings at
Rattle Brook Head to meet commercial demand for peat
products certainly pre-dated railway. Packhorse transport
succeeded by horse-drawn cart, then by standard-gauge railway
for horse-traction, 1879; this necessitated walkway; a few RBPR
granite sets, removed when laying sleepers for locomotive
traction before World War I, still seen near trackbed. Line
reached foot of Dartmoor at Noddon Gate, only ¾-mile
(1.2km) from Bridestowe Station on LSWR line
(Exeter–Okehampton–Lydford–Tavistock–Plymouth: built
1874), yet RBPR needed 1½ miles (2.4km) to negotiate gradient
from Noddon Gate to Bridestowe, where granite loading
platform and main-line siding built. This true mountain railway,
reaching 1,800ft (549m) on Rattlebrook Hill (1,050ft (320m)
above Bridestowe Station), approached station by level crossing
on A386 near main-line underbridge. Peat carried from
Amicombe Hill turf ties to nearby works by man-propelled,
narrow-gauge tramroad trucks – a method common in mines
and quarries until recent times. During World War I, two petrol-
driven trolleys purchased, built in Okehampton by Day & Sons;
larger hauled one or two trucks carrying casks of distilled peat,
smaller used for track maintenance. Taylor Bros manufactured
a black anti-frostbite ointment from distillation; exported to
British troops in Russia. Distilled peat also exported to continent
until late 1920s. Railway used, as at Red Lake, for conveying
employees and freight to and from works.

Most writers give 1931–2 as date of dismantling railway; yet
in November 1935, The Holford Processes Ltd of 74 Coleman
Street, London EC4, informed Devon County Council re:

76

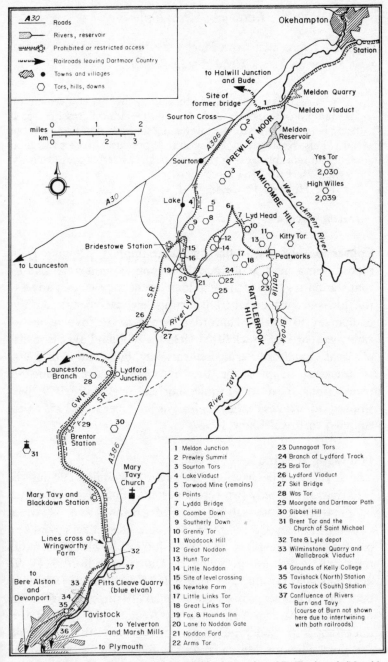

miles 0   1   2
km 0   1   2   3

Okehampton

Station

to Halwill Junction and Bude

Meldon Quarry

Site of former bridge

Meldon Viaduct

Sourton Cross

1

Meldon Reservoir

PREWLEY MOOR

2

Yes Tor 2,030

High Willes 2,039

Sourton

3

AMICOMBE HILL

West Ockment River

Lake   4

5

6

7 Lyd Head

9   8

10

11

Kitty Tor

Bridestowe Station

12

13

15

14

16

17

Peatworks

19

18

to Launceston

20

21

24

22

SR

25

23

RATTLEBROOK HILL

Rattle Brook

26

River Lyd

27

Launceston Branch

28

Lydford Junction

GWR

SR

River Tavy

29

30

Brentor Station

31

A386

Mary Tavy Church

Mary Tavy and Blackdown Station

Lines cross at Wringworthy Farm

32

37

to Bere Alston and Devonport

33

Pitts Cleave Quarry (blue elvan)

34

35

Tavistock

36

to Yelverton and Marsh Mills

to Plymouth

1	Meldon Junction	23	Dunnagoat Tors
2	Prewley Summit	24	Branch of Lydford Track
3	Sourton Tors	25	Brai Tor
4	Lake Viaduct	26	Lydford Viaduct
5	Torwood Mine (remains)	27	Skit Bridge
6	Points	28	Was Tor
7	Lydda Bridge	29	Moorgate and Dartmoor Path
8	Coombe Down	30	Gibbet Hill
9	Southerly Down	31	Brent Tor and the Church of Saint Michael
10	Grenny Tor	32	Tate & Lyle depot
11	Woodcock Hill	33	Wilminstone Quarry and Wallabrook Viaduct
12	Great Noddon	34	Grounds of Kelly College
13	Hunt Tor	35	Tavistock (North) Station
14	Little Noddon	36	Tavistock (South) Station
15	Site of level crossing	37	Confluence of Rivers Burn and Tavy (course of Burn not shown here due to intertwining with both railroads)
16	Newtake Farm		
17	Little Links Tor		
18	Great Links Tor		
19	Fox & Hounds Inn		
20	Lane to Noddon Gate		
21	Noddon Ford		
22	Arms Tor		

Map 11 GWR: Tavistock (South) – Lydford Junction; SR: Tavistock (North) – Okehampton; Rattlebrook Peat Railway

negotiated agreement with Duchy of Cornwall for lease of peat beds at Rattle Brook Head together with:

> ... a disused railway which terminates at Bridestowe on the Okehampton–Plymouth road. At one time a level crossing was in being between the terminal point and a siding at Bridestowe station yard. This crossing we do not wish to re-open and in place thereof to erect a suitable bridge over the road to take a narrow gauge railway. (Signed) H. HOLFORD
> for The Holford Processes Ltd.

Devon Record Office

Conversion of track to narrow gauge implied, presumably by repositioning one side of track throughout. Quant states (*Notes*) that standard gauge facilitated loan by SR to peat company 4–5 ton, low-sided wagon for transporting new machinery and heavy equipment to works. Holford scheme last to involve use of railway: abortive. Track lifted 1936–7: William Lavis, formerly of Great Crandford Farm, confirms date. Following World War II trackbed adapted for use by lorries. Last commercial transactions: peat to Torquay horticultural firm 1955; peat shipped to wholesale horticulturists in Guernsey 1955; peat supplied to Royal Show 1956.

Following the line
The direction of description follows the descending line and the walker will need only two verbal permits of passage; these must be obtained before setting out: Mr Brian Lavis of Great Crandford Farm (OS ref: 525879) would like walkers to make a personal call at the farm, and Mrs J. Lake of Newtake Farm (OS ref: 528870) will accept telephone requests (Lydford 314). *No dogs* may be taken through their fields. To follow the railway in both directions means a walk of 12 miles (19km) on a hard, stony track. The wise course is to enjoy treading the springy turf underfoot from Noddon Gate in a direct line to the peat works (see dotted line on Map 11), and to follow the railway on the return, so reducing the overall distance to 9 miles (14.5km).

The walk to Rattle Brook Head involves a climb of 1,000ft (305m); a map is necessary unless the walker intimately knows the ground – and good visibility is a *sine qua non*. A car may be driven up the lane behind the Fox & Hounds Inn and parked at Noddon Gate. From the gate, follow the stony track beside the wall (right) and descend to Noddon Ford. Cross the River Lyd and follow the track ahead to the north foot of Arms Tor; the tor further to the walker's right, surmounted by the painter Widgery's memorial cross for Queen Victoria's Jubilee, is Brai (pronounced 'Bray') Tor (misnamed 'Brat Tor' on OS maps). If the track seems indistinct after passing Arms Tor, steer left across dry heathery ground towards the mass of Great Links Tor. From this lofty pile – from where both English and Bristol Channels are visible – steer north-eastward across an elevated plain – the terrain rather rough, peaty and wet – towards the distant, skyline protuberance of Kitty Tor on the long ridge of Amicombe Hill. The plain is succeeded by the descent to Rattle Brook Head; if a true line has been maintained between Great Links and Kitty Tors, the ruined peat works will come into view and the walker will gradually converge with the railway, left. The rock-pile seen a short way beyond the railway is Hunt Tor, under Woodcock Hill. A considerable amount of masonry and metal remains at the works, a strange anomaly in this remote marshy basin between the long sweep of Amicombe and the Dunnagoat Tors; the gaunt gable of Bleak House downstream in the Rattle Brook Valley seems only to enhance the melancholy of the scene.

Leaving the works, the ascending railtrack crosses Rattlebrook Hill (the peaty plain east of Great Links Tor) with the old works in view until, reaching the end of a shallow cutting, it curves north-west to commence its long descent; here occurs a dramatic scenic change beyond Great Noddon where, many hundreds of feet below, an unending patchwork of fields stretches deep into north Cornwall. On this and other stretches of the line are seen wooden sleepers, often irregularly spaced. A direct descent now leads to the upper Lyd Valley, where Lydda Bridge carries the railway across the infant river, here only $\frac{1}{2}$

Plate 13 Rattlebrook Peat Railway – the trackbed descending to the works. In the centre are the ruined works, after demolition in 1961. Top right are peat ties on Amicombe Hill. The parallel lines between the ties and the ruins are narrow-gauge tramways for man-hauled trucks

mile (0.8km) below its source in Tiger's Marsh. The ruin of a medieval tinners' house lies beside the track (left) near the bridge. From the river bank one may see the embankment superstructure on the bridge – basically a clapper – to maintain railroad level, an expedient far less troublesome and costly than building a bridge on high piers. Look down the wild Lyd Valley from here and notice everywhere the workings of the medieval tinners who built the 'house' beside the stream as their shelter.

A track from the south-east converges with the railway at Lydda Bridge; this is an old peat road to Kitty Tor which, ascending from Southerly Gate, passes over Lydda Bridge, behind Grenny (OS 'Gren') Tor and Hunt Tor, and fords Rattle Brook near its head springs. Beyond the bridge the railway continues north-westward to the junction known to the moormen as 'Points'. Whereas in such places a mountain road executes a hairpin bend, a railway, of its nature, must curve on a reasonable radius; available hillside space forbade this, and the problem was solved by the laying of a forked junction controlled by points. When horses were used, trains were hauled beyond the points on to line B, where the team was unhitched and rehitched at the opposite end of the train. The points then being switched, the haul could continue from A to C, or *vice versa*. When mechanical locomotion replaced horses, no position change for the engines was necessary, as each was equipped with a gearbox giving a reverse speed equal to forward gear. Points and the approaching trackbed above and below may be seen from Little Links Tor. From Points, the outline of Great Links Tor is impressive, and Great Noddon, which appears insignificant from the ridge of Rattlebrook Hill, becomes assertive in the downward view.

On Southerly Down a bridge carries the line across a once much-used moorland track; one of three overbridges on the line, it is still intact and was relaid with heavy timbers after World War II to take the weight of laden lorries. A shallow cutting soon follows on the west slope of Great Noddon and a miniature wooden bridge constructed to carry the line over a culvert. The bridge planks contain the holes of the rail-fixing bolts as sleepers, of course, were not needed on the bridge. At a much lower elevation is seen the trackbed of the old SR leading to the impressive Lake Viaduct. Sleepers on this stretch of the RBPR are consistently 6ft (1.8m) apart, and below the cutting is a plain affording fine views of western Dartmoor. Also visible from here, 150ft (46m) down the west hillside and parallel with the railway, is the King Way, the ancient coach road between Tavistock and Okehampton. Bordering the west edge of the plain is a long embankment, actually the waste tip of soil taken from the cutting next down-line. Near it and beneath its shelter are the remains of two buildings; the first contains a stationary-engine bed with fixing bolts still in place, and the second, once roofed with corrugated iron, has a fireplace. In the succeeding cutting is a rock containing a series of drilled holes, some containing metal pegs which appear to be broken drill-bits (rather than mason's tares). The rock protrudes from the side of the cutting and was probably prepared for blasting and then declared a non-hazard. At the foot of the cutting the line approaches its first gateway and enters the enclosed lands. Armed with the requisite permission, therefore, climb the gate and follow the embankment to Newtake Farm, its modern barn conspicuous beside the railway. (The building seen left is the Fox & Hounds Inn.) Pass through a gateway near the farm (below and left of the line) and enter the Great Crandford fields. Walk into the Newtake farmyard; regain the track beyond it, where it was carried by a now dismantled overbridge across a farm track. The piers of the bridge are of slate, with well-set granite quoins. The line now descends rather more steeply and enters a short cutting; sleeper impressions are clear in the softer ground here, and upon emerging from the cutting the walker will see that he is only one field distant from the main (A386) road; beyond it, now very near, are the buildings of Bridestowe Station and a beautiful pastoral view, sheep-studded in lambing time, spread out in the west. As the line follows a level below the cutting – a scene overlooked by the huge lump of Great Noddon in the east – the railway executes a long curve to reach the station. An embankment, in places 20ft (6m) high, carries the line to within a short distance of the high road where, again, a level is reached; still standing here are the decaying crossing gates which once swung across the main road during the locomotive era of the line. The railway now converges with the main SR trackbed, which arrives here from the road overbridge near the level crossing. About 150yd (46m) down the RBPR track are the remains of the granite loading platform, with iron bolts remaining in the masonry; beyond it is the trackbed of the original LSWR siding, now very overgrown, its junction with the main line being just north of the station. Standing on the decayed loading platform, where once casks of distilled Rattle Brook peat were transferred to main-line wagons for their long journey to Russia, one can appreciate the surveying expertise behind the construction of the RBPR, for two tiers of its serpentine ascent of the Dartmoor escarpment are visible – one in the Great Crandford fields and the other, nearly 400ft (122m) higher, on the shoulder of Great Noddon.

The winter and spring climate on the north-west fringe of Dartmoor is severe, and prolonged frost used to prohibit the cutting of peat and the use of the railway for weeks at a time.

9
GWR: Marsh Mills, Plympton–Tavistock (South)

12 miles (19.3km)   Map 12

Historical digest

Tavistock, although important ore-mining centre 100–150 years ago, was remote, needing efficient communication means, to supersede packhorses and horse-drawn wagons, to expanding port of Plymouth. During early 1850s rival companies competed to build railway; South Devon & Tavistock Railway Company successful 1854, supported by Earl of Morley; line needed heavy engineering work, opened 21 June 1859. Great engineer Isambard Brunel engaged during construction to succeed deceased presiding engineer; result: 6 remarkable timber viaducts on granite piers and 3 tunnels: 5 of former replaced 1893–1910 by all-stone structures; 6th, Grenofen, demolished 1965. Line extended to Lydford and Launceston 1865. SDTR absorbed by GWR 1878; conversion of gauge from broad to standard May 1892. Line notably scenic; use declined during early post World War II years; closed as uneconomic 1962; track lifted 1964.

Following the line

At Marsh Mills, Plympton, just east of the rail-over-river bridge, was Tavistock Junction, where the line branched northward from the main Exeter route and passed beneath the Plympton road. The name 'Marsh Mills' denoted the former large flour mill east of Longbridge. The mid-nineteenth-century mill owners were quick to take advantage of rail transport as the system grew. Beyond the bridge are the platforms of the former Marsh Mills Station, opened to passengers on 15 March 1861 and closed 101 years later. A car may be parked at the roadside near the station approach gate. Land has been leased, further up-line, both by British Rail and English China Clays, to the

84

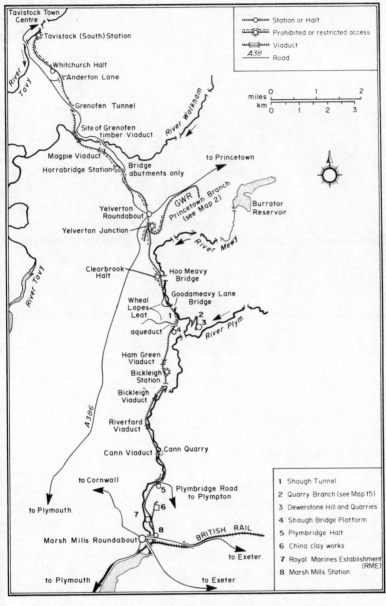

Tavistock Town Centre

Tavistock (South) Station

Whitchurch Halt

Anderton Lane

River Tavy

Grenofen Tunnel

River Walkham

Site of Grenofen timber Viaduct

Magpie Viaduct

Horrabridge Station

Bridge abutments only

to Princetown

GWR Princetown Branch (see Map 2)

Burrator Reservoir

Yelverton Roundabout

Yelverton Junction

River Meavy

Clearbrook Halt

Hoo Meavy Bridge

Goodameavy Lane Bridge

Wheal Lopes Leat

aqueduct

River Plym

1 2
3
4

Ham Green Viaduct

Bickleigh Station

Bickleigh Viaduct

River Tavy

A386

Riverford Viaduct

Cann Viaduct   Cann Quarry

to Cornwall

Plymbridge Road to Plympton

5

7   6

to Plymouth

8

BRITISH RAIL

Marsh Mills Roundabout

to Exeter

to Plymouth

to Exeter

1 Shaugh Tunnel
2 Quarry Branch (see Map 15)
3 Dewerstone Hill and Quarries
4 Shaugh Bridge Platform
5 Plymbridge Halt
6 China clay works
7 Royal Marines Establishment (RME)
8 Marsh Mills Station

Map 12 GWR: Marsh Mills, Plympton – Tavistock (South)

85

Plate 14 What are they waiting for? (The track is a length relaid on the old Tavistock line near Marsh Mills.) See Plate 15

Plym Valley Railway Association, who are restoring the track for steam haulage as far, initially, as Plymbridge Halt, with the intention of extending the line to Bickleigh in the foreseeable future. Clearance of the trackbed began in 1981 and the line can be followed from the woods beside the Royal Marines Establishment, the depot built in 1939 for the Royal Ordnance Corps preceding the RME. Discouraging notices about guard-dogs appear inside the fence opposite the level-crossing gates beyond the station and it is sensible not to follow the track literally, but to rejoin it in the wood beside the RME, from where one may look back at the junction with the branch lines, one to the china-clay works, the other to the RME. There is, in any case, an element of trespass and danger in walking beside the permanent way, for freight traffic still travels both sidings.

The GWR enters the woods at a slightly higher level than the LMT, and the permanent way remains in place as far as a buffer stop opposite the RME. Just south of this point is the site for the new PVR station. The old fences remain on either side of the continuing trackbed for much of the way and a rock cutting some 30ft (9.1m) deep is succeeded by a bridge over the Cann Canal; that the height of this would not permit the passage of canal boats shows that any intention of extending the navigable canal to a wharf at Plympton was abandoned by 1854, when the railway was built. After crossing the deep little valley in Shearwood Plantation the line curves to enter Woodford Wood. Here occurs the Lee Moor Crossing (see p32) where the LMT, which runs up-line from Plympton between the high river bank and the GWR, crosses the latter to approach the Plymbridge road viaduct and Cann Wood inclined plane. Views across the river and valley floor on this stretch of line are beautiful, especially in autumn, when the woodlands on each side are draped in gold. At Plymbridge Halt, opened in 1906, a few relics remain of GWR days, and a path descends to the Plymbridge road, where a spacious car park exists west of the bridge.

The locality of Plymbridge offers much to those who appreciate woodland scenery. Of interest, too, are the parallel

Plate 15 The arrival of British Rail Standard Class 4 4–6–0, No 75079 (to be renamed *City of Plymouth*, 16 March 1982 (see Plate 14)

lines of communication here – in order west to east, the Leigham road, the river, the PDR, GWR, Cann Canal and LMT – six lines in all. The GWR, crossing the Plymbridge road on a single-arch stone bridge, enters Tower Wood, where it follows a valley-side shelf below a steeply cut cliff, right. This gives way to a deep hollow containing ribbons of running water, which flow through a culvert beneath the embankment; cataracts occur in the river, left, making this stretch of line highly picturesque. Near Cann Quarry the line enters a cutting and passes below a bridge carrying a lane to Cann Cottages; signs exist near the bridge to suggest that slate from the quarry was once loaded on SDTR trucks here. Relics appear (right) of Cann Cottages and on both sides of the river of the former quarry workings. Here the line crosses the valley on its first high-level bridge, Cann Viaduct; this, notably sound except for crumbling coping, is 127yd (116m) long, 63ft (19.2m) high, and its original wooden span was replaced by granite in 1907. The River Plym rolls noisily between the piers below and the glorious autumn woods rise like curtains to a great height above the valley floor; a ruined waterwheel pit near the north end and remains of buildings at the south end of the viaduct dispel any notion that the peace of the woods remained unshattered a century ago. Today one hears only birds, the forester's saw and the rolling river.

Across the valley from Cann Viaduct comes a clear view of the PDR main line in Colwill Wood and of the old quarries there. The GWR, reaching the west bank of the river, has now to cross the same tributary valleys as the PDR 100ft (30m) above it, but with the difference that these greatly gain in width as they fall and necessitate either lofty viaducts or immense embankments pierced by culverts. Walking up-line, one passes a precipitous rock wall, left, and a steep drop to the valley floor, right. Beyond a small ledge, from which one may admire the beautiful Plym below, another embanked valley crossing occurs where a stream dashes to the river, next a fine old bridge of blue Cann slate carrying a quarry track that zig-zags to the valley floor, then another bridge, one of tubular iron on granite piers; this also once served a quarry, but private ground at the upper end of the truncated track and Alsatian guard dogs, released on the slightest pretext, should dissuade any walker from attempting to pass here between the GWR and PDR. The railroad now approaches the 'glen' of Glen Holt, which it crosses on Riverford Viaduct into Henroost Wood. Much cutting and embanking was necessary here to bring it to Bickleigh Viaduct in Cann Wood, from where a wet and muddy stretch leads to the lofty bridge above the road between village and Bickleigh (river) Bridge. Beyond the tubular bridge the track is spanned by a fence and stile, and a notice-board shows that from Cann the line has passed through Plymbridge Woods, owned by the National Trust. Riverford Viaduct is in excellent condition; built entirely of granite, including the parapet coping, in 1893, it is 127yd (116m) long and 97ft (29m) high. It is satisfying to look up the subsidiary valley from here to the interlocking spurs of the hills above; these, although covered mostly by coniferous woods, make a fine picture. From the east parapet may be seen in some detail the Royal Marines' 42 Commando Establishment at Bickleigh. In Henroost Wood the line crosses another subsidiary valley on a high embankment with culvert. Shortly afterwards comes Bickleigh Viaduct, no less than 123ft (37m) above the river. Three stone viaducts occur on this line within a distance of $1\frac{1}{3}$ miles (2.1km) – Cann, Riverford, Bickleigh – and a fourth – Ham Green – in just under a further mile (1.6m). Bickleigh village and church make an attractive picture from the west parapet of the bridge, while the moorland heights of Shiel Top and Pen Beacon loom above the east side.

As commonly occurs, cutting succeeds viaduct and, except for one swampy patch, walking is easy, with the sound of the river rising constantly from below. A good path leaves the trackbed, right, and climbs to the roadside at Bickleigh road-bridge (where there is space only for one car). Dumping has taken place here with unsightly results. As the cutting declines and bushes and thickets vanish, a wire-fenced farm track crosses the line; this is followed immediately by Bickleigh Station, now on private land attached to Rose Cottage, where permission must be sought to visit the station. Platforms are intact, and as the line approaches the station a nearby residence named 'The Coach House' may be noted as the former stationmaster's house. The line is completely overgrown as far as the Shaugh road-bridge; therefore, park near the bridge and observe from the roadside gate the continuing trackbed leading to Ham Green Viaduct. The gate is kept locked and has a notice forbidding entry to private land. This is the property of the Maristow Estate, and the gate has been padlocked and wired because of the crumbling coping on Ham Green Viaduct. Mrs M. Mason, agent at the estate office, is willing to consider requests to pass through the gate, but it will entail a personal call at the office (Maristow Estate Office, Roborough, Plymouth) with a copy of this book as proof of the walker's bona fide intentions. Vandals have thrown down much of the viaduct coping and access therefore has to be controlled.

The gate mentioned opens upon the old Bickleigh coalyard and the first notable feature beyond it is Ham Green Viaduct; beside it, and now of archaeological interest, are the surviving slatestone piers of Brunel's vanished wooden viaduct. The granite replacement, built in 1899, is 190yd (174m) long, 91ft (28m) high and allows impressive views across border-country woodlands to the rocky summit of Dewerstone Hill on Dartmoor's edge. Above the west parapet, and now quite near, is the Royal Marines Establishment. Good walking follows through Ham Green Plantation, Hele Lane Bridge comes in sight and the stone-built Shaugh Bridge Platform lies immediately below it. A siding had existed at Shaugh – later superseded by the passenger platform – since the line was constructed; it was installed for loading iron ore from Shaugh Bridge Iron Mine. The halt, like that at Plymbridge, had heavy use before the motor age at weekends and holiday times by Plymothians setting out to walk on Dartmoor – but despite concerted representation, there was no provision for passengers until 1907. A level vehicular approach, right, opens into Hele Lane. As the line continues through Grenoven Wood, it passes beneath a tubular iron aqueduct on stone piers; this relic of mid-nineteenth-century mining days was built to carry the leat from Hoo Meavy Weir across the railway to Wheal Lopes. Beyond it is the granite portal of Shaugh Tunnel, its brick-lined interior obviously in good condition: with a length of 308yd (282m), it is the shortest of the line's three tunnels.

At the north end of the tunnel are interesting views across deep pools in the River Mewy (OS 'Meavy'). The Wheal Lopes leat is again seen here, arriving beside the railway from the hillside above Goodameavy Lane. Beside the river (right) is a stone bridge-pier; none appears on the opposite bank, but a high embankment rises beyond, in line with the pier, all being relics of the Dewerstone Quarry branch line (see Chapter 10). No difficulties present themselves until well after Goodameavy Lane bridge (intact) is passed. As Clearbrook Halt (1928–62) is approached, the platforms are seen to languish behind a barbed-wire barricade, and washing sometimes flutters in the breeze where once the north-bound locomotive waited. Leave the track, therefore, and climb the steep hillside, left; reaching a hillside path, follow it towards the roofs of nearby houses and join a metalled road at the foot of Clearbrook Common; turn right opposite the village hall and descend the hill past cattle-grid and railway bridge (intact). The railroad north of the bridge is badly overgrown and leads into private fields and woods; proceed, therefore, as follows.

Leaving the car at the riverside near Hoo Meavy Bridge, follow the upstream riverside track westward until some old mine workings are passed (the railway embankment is in the woods above, left) and Yeoland House comes in sight. Leaving the private drive right, ascend the path (left) through the wood converging with the railway. Pass through a white wicket gate where a notice reads, 'Please keep to the path'; it is certainly advisable to do this in either direction, for the walking is easy and the railway never out of sight. The path affords good views beyond the fine old longhouse of Elfordtown Farm to the Dartmoor border heights and brings the walker into Elfordtown Lane (between the farm and Yelverton) where the bridge also is intact. For some considerable way it is not possible actually to walk the trackbed, but it can be followed in close proximity.

From Elfordtown Lane bridge to the south end of Yelverton

Tunnel – which passes beneath St Paul's Church and Yelverton Roundabout – and including the relics of the station, the line passes through the property of Col C. R. Spencer. No railway line must ever pass here again, for it would destroy something far more rare and tangible than steam nostalgia; the Colonel has spent twenty years in developing the site as a nature reserve, with special regard to *Lepidoptera*, his particular interest. My son and I were conducted to every corner of the reserve by Colonel Spencer, who asks me here to emphasise that there is absolutely no admittance to any part of the reserve without the owner's personal permission and guidance. The butterflies and birds in this post-steam sanctuary are a joy, and it would be difficult to envisage a better use for an old station site. Platforms remain, including that of the Princetown bay, as it was known, although the original station of 1885 was destroyed by fire twenty years later. Col Spencer pointed out a path – it has always been a private one – leading to Elfordtown House from the station, where the porter used to trundle his barrow-load of luggage for train-borne guests in bygone days. South of the platforms is a siding, where, during the last war, truck-loads of rubble were brought up and unloaded from bomb-scarred Plymouth; nearby is the base of a hut, still containing fireplace with grate, also an equipment shed from which gear was transported by manually propelled rail trolley to any part of the line required. Between the main line and diverging Princetown branch lay an inspection pit and turntable, the latter installed especially for turning a snow-plough to head where needed – and used also, of course, by the Princetown branch locomotives; the plough was based at the Laira depot and had often to clear the line in the Yelverton area, where it climbs to 630ft (192m) in the Dartmoor border-country, to say nothing of the gradual ascent of the branch to more than double that height at Princetown. G. H. Anthony writes in *The Tavistock, Launceston & Princetown Railway* that Yelverton became a busy station before World War I, with a bookstall and a forecourt busy with horse-drawn carriages conveying passengers to and from trains; also that, beautified by roses and rhododendrons, its condition was a matter of pride to the staff 'and the delight of the commuters'.

Continuing up the lane to Yelverton the walker must bear in mind that he is following a private road, not a public right of way, and that no attempt must be made to drive a car along its upper portion between Yelverton and the old station. It also is advisable to apply in writing to Colonel Spencer (Elfordtown, Yelverton, Devon) if it is proposed to conduct a walking party along this road. I make no apology for reminding readers that the owners of land adjoining, or over which passes, a disused railway do suffer an unjustifiable degree of annoyance from enthusiasts who pay scant regard to their privacy. Also within the nature reserve are the deep cutting approaching the 641yd (586m) long tunnel and the embankment carrying the Princetown branch trackbed in a northward curve.

The next phase of railroad exploration is less straightforward than the last, and a car is practically indispensable. Two bridges (one only intact) carry the line across two lanes successively branching north from Harrowbeer Lane (which leaves Yelverton Green beside the Rock Methodist Church). Part of the embanked trackbed here is owned by Miss P. Tutton, who used often to travel over the line and greatly misses the sight and sound of the trains. At North Road, a northward turning from the main A386 beyond the Retreat Hotel, the overgrown trackbed can be viewed from the underbridge parapet. Private gardens, sheds and greenhouses encroach upon the line north of Yelverton Tunnel — except on Miss Tutton's piece of trackbed — and in other places gorse and trees block progress; it is therefore wise to drive straight to Horrabridge Station from the North Road bridge. Pass between the abutments of the overbridge; turn left into the station entrance, where a gated level crossing gave access also from Horrabridge Hill on the south side. In the great mining days of the last century, large quantities of copper ore from local mines were loaded on train at Horrabridge for shipment at Plymouth. Ores from the mines in pre-SDTR days went by wagon to Tavistock and onward by Tavistock Canal barge to Morwellham, a process immeasurably slower than direct rail-to-ship transport via Plymouth. During February

1860, for instance, over 200 tons of copper ore were despatched from Horrabridge Station. Two commercial firms now occupy the station site, whose managers are pleased to admit walkers, on request, to see the old station. Platforms, cattle-bay and two buildings remain; the first building houses the offices of Weston Agriculture Ltd, the approach being the original platform ramp and steps, and the second, together with the coal siding, maintains historic continuity through its occupation by coal merchants W. E. Harvey & Son Ltd. From the fence at the end of their property may be seen the shallow cutting carrying the line through private land in Harwood Plantation, where a bridge has lost its span and a long cutting follows through solid elvan.

Beyond the broken bridge an embankment brings the line to the lofty Magpie Viaduct, all three features being BR property; the viaduct, however, is crumbling and consequently blocked and wired up at each end. Heathland rises above the west side of the viaduct to Alston Moor, while streams and shining bogs below feed the River Walkham. The walking beyond this is easy enough; leave the car in the park at Bedford Bridge, walk through the wooden fence and cross a bridge over a streamlet. Take the steeper (left) of two paths ahead, cross an old leat channel and mount the hillside until the railway is seen. Turn left and walk to the viaduct; notice the fine view of Leedon and Sharp Tors and Peak Hill. Walk northward. Passing an underbridge, the walker receives a surprise: on the brink of a bridgeless valley, where the vigorous Walkham flows 150ft (45m) below, the line apparently vanishes into thin air. Stand and regard. Stone work, crumbling and overgrown, remains on each side of the trackbed. In direct line, beyond the river, a rush-filled cutting leads to the granite portal of a tunnel. The missing link was the only surviving Brunel timber viaduct on the line; said to have been the finest example of its type, it was 132ft (40m) high and 367yd (335m) long. Brunel's wooden cantilevers were replaced by iron in 1896. The viaduct, which, as Anthony observes, 'had great beauty and fitted gracefully into the local landscape', was destroyed as redundant in 1965; how well worth preservation it would have been deemed today! The portal seen is

Fig 1 Grenofen Viaduct

that of Grenofen Tunnel, which passes beneath the A386 road
and the Halfway House Inn to emerge into Tavy country a mile
(1.6km) south of Whitchurch.

Beneath the shadow of the viaduct was the nineteenth-century
Gem Mine, where moss-covered ruins, pits, tips, leats and
dressing floors on the river's right bank rest among silent,
encroaching woodland. The River Walkham flows timelessly
past these decaying memorials to man's effort. Above Bedford
Bridge ½ mile (0.8km), and 100yd (91m) before a drive entrance
(left), is an iron gate (left); the track from it zig-zags down the
hillside to reach the river at the site of the viaduct piers. Gate,
track and riverside are the property of the West Devon Borough
Council who are willing to allow one or two walkers at a time to
mount the gate (it remains padlocked) and follow the track to the
riverside. The Council's permission must be sought, however, for
a party to follow this route. (Write to The Chief Executive and
Secretary, West Devon Borough Council, Kilworthy Park,
Drake Road, Tavistock, Devon, PL19 0BZ.) Grenofen Tunnel,
blocked to prevent entry, is 374yd (342m) long and dead
straight; it opens northward opposite Ash Farm (on the
Horrabridge–Tavistock road), from where the line may be
followed without difficulty as far as Anderton Lane,
Whitchurch. It is best, however, to start walking at the further

95

point by driving to Anderton Court, a turning off Anderton Lane into a modern housing estate. Park. Walk through a gateway between the rear of Whitchurch Methodist Chapel (1861, thus post-dating the line) and the railway, where once a level crossing to farm fields existed. Walk southward to the mouth of Grenofen Tunnel. Returning to Anderton Lane, notice the houses of nearby Whitchurch and those of Tavistock town beyond, set within a ring of surrounding hills. Dense thickets and gorse grow on Anderton Lane bridge and the embankments on either side. Therefore, drive to the Whitchurch Service Garage, turning left into a wide space beside the next bridge (span removed), where the noisy little Tiddy Brook flows to join the Tavy. Follow the line, left, behind the housing terrace by ascending the granite ramp of Whitchurch Halt platform and continue to the abutment of Anderton Lane bridge, so completing another link in the railroad's course. Mrs M. A. Mudge, who lives beside the halt, told me that the original wooden platform and steps near the bridge disappeared during reconstruction in the 1930s. The platform, with a curve pleasing to the eye, was packed with sightseers on the last day of operation (29 December 1962), when up-trains were prevented by snowdrifts from reaching Launceston. The locomotive heading the last down-train bore a large floral wreath on its smoke-box door. A friend of Mrs Mudge, Mr William Bray of Whitchurch, was a GWR permanent way inspector and carried out his duty by walking the entire line to Marsh Mills at a stretch, using a train only for his return home.

North of the bridge the embankment has in part been removed (behind Whitchurch Service Garage), and the cutting that once followed it has been in-filled for the building of a housing estate. The next embankment, however, accessible for a short way is interrupted by a spanless bridge where a narrow lane once led to Wheal Crelake. To see this last accessible stretch of line, drive to Pixon Lane and park in the wide open space, left, near the railway embankment. Ascend this and walk southward, passing over the asphalted trackbed leading to a depot of the Royal Corps of Transport. At the depot gates, the railway continues as a lawn-like plain of some width to the north abutment of the Crelake Lane bridge. A siding existed here for Crelake Mine, which in later times was used for the Tavistock gasworks, coal being transported to the works from the high embankment by a gravity chute. Return northward to Pixon Lane bridge (intact), where the way is barred by a wire-mesh fence; visible through it is the line of the trackbed and the wall of Tavistock Cattle Market. You have arrived at Tavistock (South) Station; opened 22 June 1859, it was burnt down in the same year as Yelverton Station (1887), rebuilt of stone, and received its last passengers on 29 December 1962. The bridge over Pixon Lane is owned by Fairey Winches Ltd, whose establishment occupies the site of the station buildings. Behind the factory, but now asphalted, are the trackbeds of up-line and cattle siding, the latter directly serving the market. Standing in the car-turning space beyond Fairey's entrance gate, it is simple to align the track of the line with the abutment of the bridge behind the Abbey Garage on the further side of Whitchurch Road; here runs the trackbed of the later built continuation of the line to Lydford and Launceston. Considerable quantities of freight were handled at Tavistock before road transport became a competitive threat following World War II. Ore from the mines, formerly sent by the Tavistock–Morwellham Canal, has already been mentioned; added to this were large amounts of merchandise and numerous travellers between the military camp (now demolished) on Plaster Down and Plymouth. Goods marshalling at Tavistock (South) Station was done mostly between 1am and 5am and a strict rule in operation during SDTR days limited the number of laden trucks to 28 per train between Tavistock and Plymouth and the speed to 20mph (32kph). The station was the only one on the line to have the protection of an all-over roof. Its final freight consignment was loaded on 7 September 1964.

10
GWR: Dewerstone Quarry Branch (Mineral Line)

1 mile (1.6km)   Map 13

Historical digest

Dewerstone Hill granite quarried long before SDTR plan raised hopes of commercial expansion through rail transport of stone. Major obstacle to providing rail link with quarries – crossing of River Mewy; SDTR followed river's west bank, but quarries were on opposite bank, a bridge being essential to forming a rail junction near Goodameavy Bridge. Wide gate and stony track here for horse-drawn vehicles to and from quarries. High pier (right bank) and abutment (left) built for branch line bridge, with massive granite embankment to maintain level of line to short cutting 200yd (183m) east.

Following the line

Pass through the cutting south of Goodameavy Gate to a rustic gate bearing the words 'Penn's Gate'; beyond this, Dewerstone Bridge spans the noisy, steeply falling Blacklands Brook from Wigford Down on Dartmoor's edge; a waterfall and a narrow rocky course are reminiscent of a Lakeland beck, and its tumble to the brawling river below sets the seal on this lovely piece of Dartmoor border-country. On the further side of the bridge stands Dewerstone Cottage; once the counting house of the quarrying firm, with a smithy at the further end, it is now the Dewerstone Scout Centre.

It was most probably at this point that horses were intended to take over from steam locomotion, for the gradient of the continuing track increases sufficiently to make the latter impracticable; if this was in fact the case, the siting of the smithy was strategic; the standard-gauge trucks would then have received their granite loads higher up-line at the foot of the inclined plane, which could only have accommodated narrow-

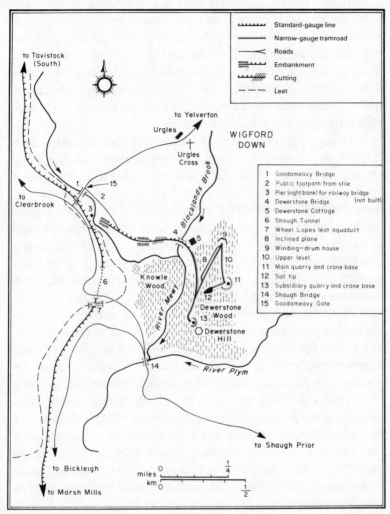

to Tavistock
(South)

to Yelverton

Urgles

WIGFORD
DOWN

Urgles
Cross

Blacklands Brook

to Clearbrook

1 Goodameavy Bridge
2 Public footpath from stile
3 Pier (right bank) for railway bridge (not built)
4 Dewerstone Bridge
5 Dewerstone Cottage
6 Shaugh Tunnel
7 Wheel Lopes leat aquaduct
8 Inclined plane
9 Winding—drum house
10 Upper level
11 Main quarry and crane base
12 Soil tip
13 Subsidiary quarry and crane base
14 Shaugh Bridge
15 Goodameavy Gate

Knowle
Wood

River Meavy

Dewerstone
Wood

Dewerstone
Hill

River Plym

to Shaugh Prior

to Bickleigh

miles   0   ¼
km   0   ½

to Marsh Mills

Map 13 Dewerstone Quarry branch (junction uncompleted) of GWR (Marsh Mills–Tavistock line) and quarry tramroad

gauge vehicles. The incline is 400yd (366m) long with a fall of 200ft (61m); this represents a gradient of 1:6, a remarkably steep one for granite-laden trucks. Trains were counterbalanced in the manner of those on the LMT inclined planes and a triple series of granite sets supported double tracks. The winding-drum house was underground; relics of the mechanism are now scant, but include one sector of a drum rim; in 1960 more remained of the two drums, including, I remember, one entire side disc. A turning bay has been excavated in the hillside near the drum-house, where horse-controlled, laden trucks from the main quarry were manoeuvred on to the inclined plane – an initial descent more gradual than the incline.

The main quarry is a grim reminder of the labour undertaken by our forefathers for wages sufficient only for the basic necessities of family life. The quarry face is about 45ft (14m) high; there is a massive crane base $18\frac{1}{2}$ft (6m) in diameter, about $3\frac{1}{2}$ft (1m) high and having a central hollow for the rotating beam of the crane. Opposite the quarry entrance is a spoil tip with high sides and comprising huge granite blocks, its 'nose' forming a precipitous spur above the steep wooded slope; it provides a particularly fine view, clearly detailed, of Knowle and Dewerstone Woods and the Mewy Valley, including the lower trackbed level and Dewerstone Cottage. The dark forms of two rock-piles, small but craggy and beetling, rise amid the trees near the quarry tip; the oaks in themselves are striking, some of them bearing epiphytes and as stunted and wizened as those in Dartmoor's Wistmans Wood. They resemble those, too, in being sheltered by the clitter of a tor – in this case the weathered rocks of Dewerstone Hill, which lie teeming on the valley side below. A few ashes, rowans and hawthorns lining the upper fringe of the wood have in general achieved a growth more normal than the oaks. As for the quarry tip, it would appear that tramroad trucks were used, a carefully made level starting from the crane base, as does that descending the hillside to the incline head. A path continuing from the line of the tramroad beyond the quarry curves to ascend to the summit of Dewerstone Hill and passes near an old walled enclosure, probably built to impound horses employed at the quarry.

The lower of the two horizontal levels – below the incline it is neither horizontal nor level – continues to climb from the incline foot to reach a subsidiary quarry in Dewerstone Wood. A few remaining granite sets on the trackbed indicate a narrow-gauge line, and within the quarry is another crane base. A continuing cart-track beyond rounds the actual spur of the peninsula and provides a fine sight of the converging rivers, Mewy and Plym. Several grotesque rock-piles rise nearby.

Notice on the return walk to Goodameavy Bridge the broken condition of the embankment near the river; this was owing to its use as a supply source of granite in 1952, during the construction of the Tavy dam at Lopwell, Maristow. Removal of stone from the embankment was so thorough near the river that the left bank bridge abutment and 14yd (13m) of the embankment have vanished. Did the bridge, the walker will wonder, collapse before, or in consequence of the removal of the abutment? The answer is that the whole transportation project was a white elephant, and there never was a bridge. Sir Massey Lopes, owner of the land where the rail junction was to have been built, withheld permission for this final but essential stage – a girder bridge on a single granite arch. The inclined plane and upper and lower levels were used, but no standard-gauge trucks ever crossed the River Mewy to collect the granite. What stone the quarry owners succeeded in selling was consequently trundled in horse-drawn wagons along the cart-track to Goodameavy Gate, while much of the quarries' production went into the sets and sleepers for the inclined plane and railroad in the early 1850s. Dewerstone Quarries worked for about twenty years, so that more than a century has elapsed since the old winding-drums last revolved.

11
GWR: Yelverton–Princetown Branch

10½ miles (16.9km)   Map 2

Historical digest

GWR line and 160-year old PDR often regarded as identical in
route, but significant deviations occur, one of 2 miles (3.2km).
Princetown Railway Company (subsidiary of GWR) adopted PDR
track (outstanding achievement in mountain railway building)
as only feasible approach to Princetown at 1,400ft (427m);
deviations necessary to provide curves suitable for steam
locomotion. Line purchased 1881 for £22,000; by early 1882
construction progressing; *Western Daily Mercury* of 5 July
reported:

> The Princetown Railway is making rapid progress, and everything
> points to the completion of the work within a few months. The
> contractor is now using up the tramline route, and all traffic is
> consequently suspended over it. Arrangements are made, however,
> for the conveyance of granite over the new line once per month. It is
> not news that the new line absorbs the tramlines for a considerable
> distance but up to the present no thought seems to have been given
> to the fact that when the railway is finished the tram rails from the
> Rock Hotel to Cattedown will remain unconnected with the new
> line, and through a track of too little value to justify locomotive
> service over it.

PDR, although enterprising in its day, inadequate to needs of
mid-Victorian Princetown. By 1870s railway regarded as
necessity. Scheme promoted at public meeting in Princetown
1877. Increasing numbers of convicts sent to penal
establishment, necessitating more warders, families, housing.
Granite from Walkham's east valley-side quarries despatched in
road wagons to Tavistock SDR Station, but some still travelled
on old PDR tramroad. Merchandise from Princetown arrived in
carts/wagons, even by packhorses. Act of Parliament for
construction of line obtained 1878. Unfortunately, line never

profitable; losses recorded as early as 1884 continued throughout decade. Receipts fluctuated for further half-century, fading drastically in post World War II motor age. Beeching axe fell 1956; line closed 5 March. Last train had six crowded coaches, two locomotives; ceremonial occasion.

Following the line

Enter Yelverton Recreation Ground by a wicket gate at the junction of Meavy Lane and the Gratton road; walk to the south (further) hedge; above it, observe the railway embankment, left, descending to the station site, indicated by a variety of trees in the nature reserve. Return to the Gratton road and approach the bridge abutments, noticing the embankment on either side. The north embankment borders some gardens to reach the next abutments in Meavy Lane, where the stonework has been lowered to accommodate the garden of a house built on the trackbed. Below this on the north side, a parallel lane runs behind the houses of Meavy Bourne. Ask at a house fronting the lane for permission to walk the embankment, which passes through gardens; it leads to a cutting (in-filled) where more gardens appear. Next, drive along the Dousland road to Westella Garage; turn right into Kirkella Road leading, at its foot on a bend, to Southella Road. Park; walk on to the railway bridge, where the in-filled cutting with its gardens (south) and mowing grass (north) renders the bridge an anachronism. North of the grass field, below the houses of Binkham Hill, the sides of the cutting decline to the next embankment. Drive along the Dousland road and branch sharp right at Woodman's Corner into Lake Lane; stop at the first gate, left; here observe the PDR and Devonport leat together crossing the field, while at the hilltop ahead is the railway embankment and site of the next bridge. Park nearby and follow a short stretch of line on either side, the northward passing through a gateway into the compound of a transport depot where it forms the boundary of the property. Beyond the latter, the line remains beside the road to the site of Dousland Station, the station building being now a residence. The remainder of the site is occupied by a housing development, but a short piece of trackbed is visible behind a (private) fence beside the Meavy road, the turning left into Manor Park pinpointing the site of Dousland Crossing; 'Crossways Cottage' here was formerly the stationmaster's house. A shallow cutting followed – since in-filled and built upon – and the line next appears at Iron Mine Lane, where signs of Prowse's Crossing remain. A wall has been built across the trackbed on the west side of the lane, while the former Dousland Post Office and crossing-keeper's cottage are opposite, the trackbed clearly seen here as the drive to a private garage.

Drive next to the junction of the Meavy and Burrator roads, east of Dousland. Turn left, pass over a cattle-grid to enter open moorland and park (left) off the road. Climb the hillside to two adjacent gates; that on the left is on the GWR trackbed, the other the PDR. The former is padlocked as the railway approaches from a private field; it is possible to follow it only for a short way, however, before the gardens near Prowse's Crossing block it. (It is possible to walk to a second fence, beneath a double-trunked oak tree; between the roots are two granite sets from the old PDR. There also was provided, on this stretch of the line, a footpath level crossing with steps in the wall on each side: these remain.) East of the gate the railway lies on the open common, and only one small impediment to progress remains throughout to Princetown.

It is here, on Yannadon (OS 'Yennadon Down') that the lengthiest deviation occurs on the moorland stretches of the GWR and PDR lines. Trains on the latter could negotiate bends quite impassable to steam locomotives, such a bend lying near the gate to Iron Mine Lane; the GWR, however, had necessarily to follow Yannadon's contour – so affording magnificent views across Burrator Gorge – in order to climb to the shoulder of Peak Hill, and in so doing, enabled the railway company later to install a halt at Burrator, one of the most beautifully sited rail halts in all Britain. The great tors beyond the valley are reflected in the lake, which lies so naturally in this deep valley, and it comes as no surprise to learn that history has repeated itself and a lake lay here in primeval times.

To follow the line to Lowery Crossing, a convenient stage point in the walk, leave the car where it is parked, walk on the trackbed to Lowery, then return over the crest of Yannadon. On passing Burrator Halt, notice the wicket gates leading to footpaths above and below the line. The channel of the Devonport leat, seen dry elsewhere near the line, is beyond here dry no longer; conducting water from the West Dart Valley and its tributaries, formerly to Devonport Dockyard, it now discharges its burden into Yelverton Reservoir in the grounds of the Lodge at Burrator, which stands below the railway beyond the halt. Conspicuous in the view is the headland jutting into the lake on the east side, where lie the remains of the ancient Longstone manor of the Elford family. Threading the plantation above the lake, the line crosses Woodland Hill (bridge span removed) and reaches the site of Lowery Crossing; the crossing-keeper's cottage stood on the right and a plate-layers' hut left, while beyond the crossing is the beginning of what once was a deep cutting (now in-filled) over the crest of Yannadon. Follow this to a fenced wall, where no entry should be attempted; the line is seen westward from here as it leaves the cutting and is embanked to reach the bridge (span removed) on the A386 road; here the walker can rejoin it and continue unhindered to Princetown. Return to the car, therefore, and turn right into the A386 at the Burrator Inn, Dousland. A wide space exists (left) at Yannadon Cross; park the car and walk just ahead to the now visible abutments of the bridge, where the Dartmoor National Park Authority have provided a stile and flight of steps to the top of the embankment (west roadside), from where the line is seen (east) emerging from Lowery Cutting. If following the railroad in summertime, a possibility is to leave the car at Yannadon Cross, walk the whole way to Princetown and return on a Dartmoor Pony Express bus. Times are available from any Dartmoor National Park Authority Information Centre, including Princetown.

The embankment, so elevated above the border-country, permits splendid views. The PDR converges from the left – to be exact, it crosses the fields on a slightly raised embankment and reaches the GWR trackbed three gateways north of the Dartmoor National Park stile – and the trackbed is for some way common to both lines; as it curves to climb northward, a breathtaking torscape opens ahead in which the great tors of Walkham and the river far below in a hidden wooded valley make the walk memorable. Also visible are the quarries from which so much granite was train-borne to Plymouth during the nineteenth and early twentieth centuries, first by the PDR, then by the GWR – granite that went into several of London's most notable buildings. The next scheduled train stop was Ingra Tor Halt (1936), where a notice-board warned passengers to 'Beware of Snakes'. Here the trains reached the 1,000ft (305m) contour and a quarry was successfully worked for many years. The timber platform supports remain, but the name-board was long ago removed by souvenir hunters. Yestor Brook is crossed in Yestor Bottom on a granite bridge and embankment – another deviation from the old PDR – from where the line passes over a level crossing from Yestor Farm to Foggintor Quarry, the gates still standing.

The great quarries of Swell Tor (see p13), now looming east of the line, were served by a long siding, and many signs remain here of the granite industry's heyday. Northward is Great King Tor: its huge rocks, split first by nature and then by man, crown a spur overlooking the Walkham Valley, with its splendid field of Bronze Age antiquities, its medieval farms, Industrial Age quarries and, in evolutionary time-scale less than a day ago, its railway halt (1928). This, curiously, is not at Great King Tor, but near Foggin Tor and would have been better so named, being there suitably sited to serve the considerable population dependent upon the industry. The inclined plane and short siding from the main line, constructed for loading granite on rail, are on the opposite, west side of the tor.

King Tor Halt is in the heart of quarryland – an area embracing the quarries of Ingra, King, Swell and Foggin – where a siding known as 'Royal Oak' led to Foggin Tor and a cart-track west of the railway to Swell Tor. The convolutions of the line here meant that it was possible to leave the train – and it was not unknown for energetic persons to do this – at the bend north of Yestor Bottom and rejoin it at King Tor Halt, a brisk walk across the hill of some 12 minutes; indeed, the timetable allowed the train 13 minutes to climb between the halts, but only 9 minutes for the return.

Views from the line on approaching Princetown are very fine, with the head and entire moorland valley of Mewy opening in the south, and the heights of southern Dartmoor beyond. The first buildings sighted are GWR houses – including the stationmaster's house, in front of which the trackbed has become a road to serve the numerous houses since sprung up. The line bore what was literally its last train, a recovery train, on 15 October 1956, and the author photographed an earlier recovery train, loaded with fittings from Princetown Station, under King Tor on a snowy March evening in 1956. The black clouds hanging ominously over the moor seemed a fitting backdrop, on that freezing evening, to the destructive processes of Time.

It seems incredible that, at a time when post-war tourism was enormously on the increase and the numbers of visitors to Dartmoor little short of astonishing, this absolutely unique railroad should have been *dismantled*; with trends recognisably what they were, British Railways could surely have exercised patience until a body of prospective purchasers of the line had had time to formulate plans and marshal funds – but I admit that is being wise after the event! Today, in the 1980s, the Princetown line would undoubtedly have been a money-spinner. The single fare from Yelverton to Princetown in 1954 was 1s 9d – less than ten pence in today's currency. Who would not today willingly lay down fifty times that sum (still less than £5) at the booking clerk's little window for the privilege of a steam-hauled trip to Princetown if, as is still a practical possibility, the line were reconstructed from a new terminal station at Dousland, east of Prowse's Crossing!

12

GWR: Tavistock (South)–Lydford Junction and SR: Tavistock (North)–Lydford Junction

6½ miles (10.4km)   Map 11

Historical digest

Lines treated concurrently because major portion of trackbeds less than 100yd (91m) apart. At Lydford, Launceston line quits Dartmoor country, swinging westward into Cornwall; SR continues northward across moor's high western fringe to Okehampton. LSWR signed agreement 1862 with GWR and SDR not to operate beyond Okehampton (to which narrow-gauge line already planned); later rescinded to allow LSWR extension through Lydford to Bere Alston and Plymouth. Line reached Okehampton October 1871 and Lydford (single track) 1874. Passenger and freight receipts justified double track 1879, necessitating skilful adaptation of Meldon Viaduct – its six girder spans on metal lattice piers. South Devon & Launceston Railway Company's Tavistock–Lydford–Launceston line inspired by Thomas W. Woolcombe, Chairman of SDR; absorbed smaller independent lines 1869; all absorbed by GWR 1878. Launceston line opened 1 July 1865; used also by LSWR Lydford–Marsh Mills until 1890, when Tavistock North Station opened and LSWR line extended to Devonport and Plymouth; this left North Station by Kilworthy Viaduct – access now blocked.

Following the line [1]= GWR; [2]= SR

[2] Tavistock (North), its roofed footbridge in position until June 1982 when it was removed and 'donated' by West Devon Borough Council to the Plym Valley Railway Association, is open to view on the north side, but on the south the station buildings constitute a private residence. The headquarter offices of the WDBC, approached by the old north platform road from

Kilworthy Hill now occupy the site of sidings, for which the plain, here backed by a rock face, was originally levelled. On leaving the station, call at the WDBC reception desk and ask permission (referring to Mr John Richards) to follow the line to the boundary of their property. This short stretch brings the walker to the fenced approach to the bridge over Exeter Street. From it, one gains the splendid view once seen by window-gazing passengers approaching the station – the town 100ft (30m) below, the swift Tavy and the tower of the parish church of St Eustachius, and on Dartmoor the tors of Cocks, Great Steeple, North Hessary, Feather and Pu.

[1] Just beyond the river is Tavistock (South), the Lydford line clearly seen approaching the Tavy bridge. It left the station by a since dismantled bridge over Whitchurch Road (but the north-east abutment remains); together with the rocky hillside here, this forms the boundary of a public car park next to the premises of Abbey Garage Ltd. The trackbed beyond the bridge is badly overgrown for 100yd (91m) and need not be followed; the next bridge, its span also removed, carries the line over the approach track to Deerpark Quarry (where the entrance gates are closed and padlocked); the best way, therefore, of retracing the line is to park a car in Dolvin Road opposite the cemetery entrance, cross the cemetery to its further boundary and follow a path ascending to the railway embankment. Turn right and follow the line to the quarry bridge, from which the short (overgrown) stretch to South Station bridge may be seen; return and continue northward, noticing masonry buttresses to the rock face (right); beyond a cutting in Mount Tavy Road (the Princetown highway), a long bridge carried the line diagonally across both road and river, three large piers remaining in a scrapyard between road and river. On the north bank, the line is embanked through SWEB property; request permission to follow it to a bridge (intact) carrying it over a lane branching from Parkwood Road (the Okehampton highway), from where it is seen to enter a private garden; this short stretch then passes behind a garage yard before ending in a modern housing estate, where the contractors have demolished the embankment and built upon its

site. Beyond College Avenue (a turning left from Parkwood Road) it enters the lower playing fields of Kelly College; in parallel meanwhile, the SR enters the higher fringe of the beautiful school grounds, the two railways thus forming their north and south bounds.

[2] The SR, from Exeter Street Bridge, is accessible by permission of the householder at 'Leander' (first on right beyond bridge). The line is eventually blocked by a 12ft (4m) wall bounding the college grounds where 'Marwood', the headmaster's modern house, rises behind it. Return to the car and drive along Exeter Lane (continuation of Exeter Street) to the next road overbridge, noticing the line above the college buildings, right. From the south parapet of Exeter Lane Bridge the line is visible at the upper edge of the grounds; from the north parapet is seen an impassable cutting where WDBC dumping has taken place. Further along Exeter Lane are houses on the left side, of which the gardens encroach upon the railway. A descent in the lane brings it to a junction with Wilminstone Road, overshadowed by Wallabrook Viaduct, beside which is the large county-council owned, Wilminstone Quarry. The south face rises from a deep pond, but the north quarry is occupied by a firm of vehicle breakers. A car may be parked in the wide lane between them. With the quarry foreman's permission, enter the north quarry and follow the inclined plane where trucks, hauled by a stationary steam engine and cable, carried stone to a crushing plant at the head of a specially built rail siding, where the stone was loaded into hopper wagons. The site of these features may be seen at the incline head. The siding, and another at the south end of the viaduct, was built in the early 1920s. Approximately 80,000 tons of roadstone was despatched annually to North Devon for use on the roads. Some years later, the opening of roadstone quarries in North Devon reduced the demand on the Wilminstone workings, where tar macadam became a product. As this, however, had to be laid when hot, it proved more convenient to transport it direct to the working site by road, and the sidings were in consequence dismantled in September 1955. An internal tramroad of 2ft (0.6m) gauge was

in use at the quarries; for its operation, Kerr Stewart & Co built 6 miniature 0-4-2 locomotives in 1922; unfortunately, 3 have vanished completely and the remaining 3 are known to have found their way to unrecorded addresses in the Midlands.

Next drive to Vigers Hall, where permission may be had from Mr or Mrs Arthur Read to follow the line through their grounds. (Readers would proceed without permission at their own risk for large dogs roam the grounds.) First walk southward to link with Wallabrook Viaduct (beyond which is a private garden), then northward to Wilminstone Bridge (span removed). Return to Vigers Hall and drive to Wilminstone Hall, a large modern house of stone, and make a similar request to Mr or Mrs G. Medland to follow the line between Wilminstone Bridge and the high valley-side shelf above the Tate & Lyle depot. The hall was built 100 years ago by a Plymouth solicitor named Goodman who cherished the hope of commuting by train from a halt at the foot of his garden – but in vain, for it never materialised. The handsome entrance gateposts at the hall were brought from Devonport Dockyard by train. A stretch of open track in front of the house (the intended site of Goodman's 'Wilminstone Halt') reveals a detailed view of the large Pitts Cleave Quarry (GWR line) beside the River Tavy; the SR next enters a deep cutting. Reaching the hillside shelf above the Tate & Lyle depot the walker will observe that the two railways begin to converge; the next needed permit, therefore, must cover both lines, so description now returns to the lower Kelly College boundary.

[1] The original course of the GWR track, as it followed the River Tavy's west bank across the college rugby ground, has been completely obliterated by the in-filling of a cutting to provide extra ground. At the north boundary of the field the line enters a pleasant glade where, beside a weir and salmon ladder, is the head of a large-capacity leat that passes beneath the main road and enters the college grounds. This once supplied the waterwheel of a large woollen mill on the fringe of the town, worked by Devon Woolcombers, the mill building now being the premises of Farm Industries Ltd. The glade is accessible from a gap in the roadside hedge opposite the branch road to the

Wilminstone Industrial Estate; a car may be parked beside the road and the railway followed in both directions. Northward, it passes the car park of the Cottage Inn and eventually reaches an electric fence bordering the garden of Wilminstone Cottage. Return to the car and drive to the turning (right) into Pitts Cleave Quarry, now a depot of English China Clays. Dolerite, a hard compact granitic stone, has been quarried here for well over a century, and four sidings were constructed in 1922 to lead into the workings from the GWR line. Stone was despatched in the quarry company's own 20-ton hopper wagons. Ask at the office for permission to walk the line to the Wilminstone Cottage boundary (north side). Afterwards, walking northward from Pitts Cleave brings one to the River Burn bridge (span removed). The remaining short stretch to the Tate & Lyle depot may be adequately viewed from the roadside north of the quarry entrance. The trackbed is, in any case, approachable only from a private field and overgrown as it nears the road overbridge beside the depot.

[1, 2] The convergence and crossing of the lines near Wringworthy Farm makes it possible to consider them in close parallel for the remainder of this chapter. Drive to the farm and request the permission of Mr Maurice Anning to follow the lines crossing his land between the depot and the approach to Mary Tavy Station, beginning at the level crossings beyond the farmyard.

[2] Follow the SR southward to the lane overbridge above the depot. A copious spring rises in the field, right, and a bridge (intact) crosses a lane between fields, beyond which the line passes through an impressive rock cutting – one of many on this line. Numerous slots up to $3\frac{1}{2}$ft (1m) long in the rock face are signs of preparation for blasting. [1] At first, the GWR will be below, right, and the River Burn, left. Opposite the farm roofs the GWR passes through a tunnel beneath the SR at a considerable depth, its trackbed very overgrown as it leaves the river to approach the tunnel, but clearer on emergence (right). On nearing the Tate & Lyle depot the walker will see that the GWR is badly overgrown near the road-bridge, and in places

Plate 16 The Waterloo–Plymouth Express approaching Wringworthy, 27 September 1957. On the left is Mary Tavy and Blackdown Station on the Great Western line. Above is Black Down (*From* More Southern Steam *by permission of D. Bradford Barton Ltd. Photo by W. L. Underhay*)

under water; its down-line continuation to Pitts Cleave Quarry and Wilminstone Cottage are clearly seen. This now completes the retracing of the GWR from Tavistock South to Wringworthy.

[2] From the lane overbridge above the depot, return northward, facing Mary Tavy church and Gibbet Hill, with the tors of Whit, Boulters, Cocks, Little Cocks and Steeple forming a bold skyline, right. From Wringworthy level crossings the two lines appear in close proximity; the SR, however, crosses a cultivated field and passes through a (padlocked) gateway; further along, fences enclose a stretch of line in use by a farmer. Climb the padlocked gate, pass another field crossing and, on approaching the fences, descend from the embankment to the GWR. Two road overbridges for the parallel railroads shortly appear ahead; at this point look up to the SR hillside line and imagine the scene (see Plate 16). Beyond the bridges (carrying the branch road from the A386 to Mary Tavy and Blackdown Station – GWR) the relative levels of the two lines remain fairly

constant for some way and curve northward with the river's course. An ancient farm lane, steeply walled, passes beneath each line – the SR needing a bridge twice the height of the GWR's – and reaches the river at a picturesque clam (wooden footbridge), steps and ford; the valley occupied by this crystal tributary of the River Tavy has much beauty and its higher reaches under Black Down are particularly peaceful and attractive.

[1] Continue on the GWR line until a fence bars the way near Mary Tavy Station, first stop north of Tavistock and now a private dwelling. (To see Mary Tavy Station, turn left before entering the village from Tavistock; continue to the bridges and view the station from the parapets.) Both platforms remain, trodden by the first passengers on 1 July 1865 and by the last on 31 December 1962, the station having been demoted to 'halt' status on 11 August 1941.

[2] The parallel SR, its first stop further up-line, passes over land now worked by Burntown Farm, and no attempt should be made to walk northward from the bridges over either line; the link-up is easy from a point further ahead, so return to Wringworthy and drive to the west foot of Black Down by forking left at Down's Garage, Mary Tavy. Pass over a cattle-grid and park on open moorland on the crest of the Brentor road where excellent views are seen. St Michael's Church on Brent Tor appears ahead, Cocks, Pu and Sharp Tors and Peak Hill rise in the south-east, and the floor of the Burn Valley, left, easily accommodates both railways. Down-line beyond the curve near the Mary Tavy bridges are seen the roof of the Tate & Lyle depot and the deep Tavy Valley below Kelly College.

[1, 2] The best course is now a triangular walk, the railways providing its base. Descend to the foot of the moor, left, join the nearer trackbed (SR) and walk southward; some small, lightly built fences and a level crossing occur, but, using discretion, the walker is unlikely to meet with rebuff. Walk to the head of the curve (near the Mary Tavy bridges), where the SR gains height over the GWR, and continue until the bridges and Mary Tavy Station are in view. The link is completed. Return up-line,

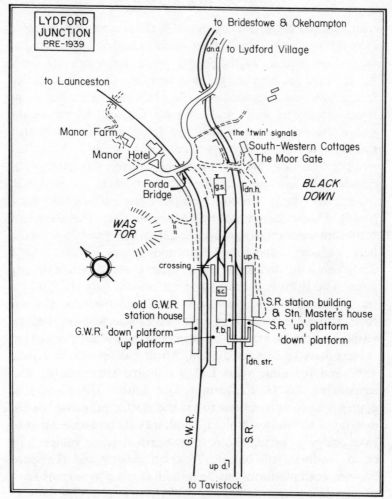

Fig 2

noticing the base of an SR plate-layers' hut complete with grate, hearth and chimney breast – somewhat forlorn without the enclosing walls. The crossing and recrossing of the River Burn by both lines causes no difficulty until, a mile (1.6km) up-line, the SR bridge is spanless. Move across, therefore, to the GWR and pass thereafter between the lines as desired, until halted after a further mile (1.6km) by a wire fence and private property on the lines 260yd (238m) ahead. This is Brentor Station (SR), which should be reached by road. On the return walk, pause to look at Wortha Mill, an old corn-grinding mill formerly in use by local farmers in an idyllic setting above the river's left bank. Again, there are twin bridges over the railroads, these separated by the river and accompanied as far as the mill by the leat to the waterwheel. The sluice and leat-head are seen higher up the valley near the private boundary fence, where several iron railway boundary posts remain: those of the 'L&SW Ry Co' are small uprights, but the 'GWR Co's Boundary 1899' is marked by circular iron discs on uprights. Also noticeable is a well-built bridge, with granite portals and parapets, and topped with a coping of elvan, carrying the SR across the river. On this stretch of line are outcrops of rock breaking from the west hillside which here rises steeply above the GWR. From the station fence, return down either line beyond Wortha Bridge to an attractive fording place. The Burn is a stream of great delight, here crossed by a track descending the flank of Black Down from the Brentor road. The walker's car, high on the valley side, will soon become visible and can be reached by ascending the hillside diagonally.

Next drive to Brentor Station, which was opened on 2 June 1890 and for some years had a full-time stationmaster and signalman. Mrs G. F. Garbutt, Old Station House, may be approached for permission to see the platforms, name-boards, exterior of the station buildings and, inevitably, another pair of twin bridges, bearing the road to North Brentor village. The down platform still has its Victorian canopy and the space between both platforms has been in-filled and planted with fruit trees. A decaying cattle-pen and buffer-stop head a siding built as early as 1866 for stock farmers and a nearby notice instructs railmen that 'Crane jibs (were) not to exceed 29 feet above Rail Level'.

Brentor Station moorgate marks the beginning of an old, much-used peat track known as the 'Dartmoor Path'. This crosses Black Down over the north shoulder of Gibbet Hill. As the Mary Tavy—North Brentor road nears the station, a branch road turns abruptly right and runs on open moorland above the enclosures, left; crossing the foot of the Dartmoor Path, it makes another abrupt bend, left, to reach the next twin bridges, here carrying Burn Lane over the railways. Near the bend are the settlements of West Blackdown, Roslyn Cottage and The Court, Burn Lane. In the last of these is the home of Hedley Walters, ex-platelayer, whose father John worked as a teenager on the construction of the LSWR in 1874. From the parapets of the Burn Lane bridges is visible a considerable length of each line, north and south. Park near the east end of Burn Lane; descend to either line from the south side of the bridges and walk southward until North Brentor Station bridges appear. Return. As complications exist near Roslyn Cottage it is pleasant to walk across the open moor in parallel with the railways as far as the gate of Burn Cottage; from here follow the wall bounding the property to the railway fences on its north side, then either track to Lydford Junction.

During Lydford's early railway years, there were two separate, independent stations, though a junction line was built soon after the opening of the LSWR station on 12 October 1874, with sidings (see Fig 2). The GWR station had been opened on 1 July 1865. Lydford became a busy station during the closing years of the last century, with much animal and tourist traffic; the Manor Hotel was built beside the station and both railways and hotel enjoyed steady custom until well after World War II. During the war, the station was regularly in use by troops exercising on Dartmoor. Also Lydford was considered a safe place for the storage of ammunition intended for services use overseas, and large quantities of explosives were secured in locked wagons shunted on to the station sidings, to be taken onwards for shipment as required. Sad to say, nothing but the platforms remain of the twin stations (and the goods-yard entrance gate). Trackbeds are swampy, with bulrushes waving in the breeze where once trains waited for the departure signal. The stations were closed, together with others on the line, on 6 May 1968. The main track and sidings layout are mostly still clear and can be studied from the parapet of the SR bridge up-line, or, better still, from the summit of the basalt crags of Was Tor above the GWR station. The view of the spread of western

Dartmoor heights is exceptional; they are, left to right: Sourton Tors, Corn Ridge, Great Noddon, the moorland Lyd Valley, Woodcock Hill, Southerly Down, Little and Great Links Tors, Arms Tor, Kitty Tor, Brai Tor, Rattlebrook Hill, Lydford Sharp Tor, Little Hare Tor, Hare Tor, Whit Hill, Black Down, Gibbet Hill; far right is Brent Tor in the border-country, while directly at the east foot of the viewpoint is the head mire of the River Burn.

13
SR: Lydford Junction–Okehampton

10½ miles (16.9km)   Map 11

Historical digest

Line opened 12 October 1874. Fine engineering achievement: included apparently frail, lattice-work Meldon Viaduct across West Ockment river; rise to Prewley Summit 950ft (289m) above sea level; succession of cuttings and embankments on Dartmoor's north-west fringe; stone viaducts of Lake and Lydford. Line failed to make century by only six years, last passenger train running 6 May 1968. Scenic merits justly celebrated – considered by many to surpass those of GWR Princetown branch.

Locomotive footplate pass enables me to describe last 2½ miles (4km) of line, in use by BR for Meldon Quarry stone trains. Directions for following line therefore end at viaduct barrier gate. Applications to visit quarry and/or walk on viaduct to: Quarry Manager, British Rail Quarries, Meldon, Okehampton, Devon.

Following the line

From the SR bridge at Lydford Junction Station the line passes through a straight cutting to an underbridge crossed by the Brentor–Lydford road. Follow it to a second bridge near Lydford village. Fences are easy to negotiate without causing damage until one of a more permanent nature is encountered. Return and fetch the car to this point, from where the walk can be continued beyond the fenced area. At the overbridge another fence occurs; *do not enter*, but return to the car. Drive to 'The Barn' (first house on the by-road beyond the bridge) and apply at the front door (furthest from entrance gate) to Commander or Mrs C. O. Lombi for permission to follow the line. Alternatively, make a pre-arrangement by telephoning Lydford 298. This is all very worthwhile, for the line passing through the garden of 'The Barn' will take the walker to the north end of Lydford Viaduct. A fine view opens from the line of Lydford church and castle, and the scene from the viaduct itself is impressive: in the east, the Lyd Valley emerges from Dartmoor under huge, looming tors, and the rushing torrent of Lyd far below is surprisingly noisy, especially on the west side, where it enters the famous Lydford Gorge. It is possible to see where the viaduct – still in perfect condition – was widened in 1878 to accommodate double track. It spans not only the river, but also a quiet country lane leading into Silver Street, an ancient way of Lydford named from the Saxon mint that stood near the site of the future Norman castle. Obstacles appearing on the line ahead are poultry houses. The space occupied is small but nevertheless private, so return to the car and drive to Bridestowe Station, from which the walker can complete the Lydford link.

At present the privately owned Bridestowe station house (with associated features) is likely to change hands and the reader must seek permission from the occupant to see the station. An open waiting shelter exists on each platform, the footbridge is intact, and of the two name-boards, one is in good condition. Flush with the platforms is a lawn with, at its north end, an unfinished swimming pool. Coal and cattle sidings are at the north end of the station, and the RBPR siding, more distant, may be inspected on the up-line walk. First pass under the road-bridge and walk southward. Several field level crossings occur, a cutting separating the first two. A tranquil valley appears below, right, and beyond it is the enclosed grassy tract of Fernworthy Down, once open heathland. A transverse valley is next, crossed by the line on an embankment, with a conduit for the streamlet trickling below to its confluence with the water from Fernworthy Down. The former greater volume of these streams is evident from the deep valleys they have excavated, forming obstacles for the railway engineer typical in West and South Devon. The workings of an old copper mine appear in the near distance at the south foot of Fernworthy Down, while equidistant to the left are the houses of Vale Down, topped by the tors of the moor's western escarpment. A waterfall in the next valley crossed by the railway creates a beautiful scene, but an overgrown cutting unpleasant to follow comes next, where dumping has taken place to a reprehensible extent. Nevertheless, the bridge next in sight means that the stretch is nearly done, for it carries the road from the Dartmoor Inn (on the A386) to Lydford village, and a short way beyond it are the poultry enclosures seen from Lydford Viaduct. The link is completed. Return, pass through Bridestowe Station (from which locally trapped rabbits were despatched to Spitalfields and Smithfield Markets), until the next overbridge is in sight. Observe a siding diverging (right) from the main line and rising slightly to reach the RBPR loading platform (see pp76, 82) from which the peat railway ascends to cross the A386. The main line, meanwhile, curves gently to pass beneath the road and into a cutting; emerging from this, the walker sees the great loop of the RBPR away to the right, backed by the upward sweep of Great Noddon. Soon the bulky outline of Sourton Tors appears ahead, and a long, deep rock cutting leads to a bridge (intact) over a stream falling from Coombe Down. The scenery onwards to Okehampton is exceedingly fine. Beyond the Coombe Down stream is the much deeper, striking incision in the moorside known as 'Deep Valley'; beside its north bank in the woods below are spoil tips of the former Torwood Copper Mine, the line crossing the stream's far-below sparkle on the splendid Lake Viaduct, approached from the Coombe Down bridge through a short rock cutting. The train passenger crossing the viaduct had time only to admire the stern aloofness of the Dartmoor scene; the foot traveller, however, can pause to take in every detail. Great Noddon's north slope, crossed by the RBPR 550ft (168m) above Lake Viaduct, appears top right; ahead is the horizon curve of Southerly Down, while left, at the head of Deep Valley, is a point known as 'Iron Catch Gate', to which the old King Way (p81) climbs before passing across the Sourton Tors—Corn Ridge col, to reappear on the railroad scene near Meldon in its descent to the border-country. The track approaching Torwood Mine from Lake hamlet is visible below, as also is the line of a leat rounding the foot of the hill, which once carried water to the mine waterwheel from the Coombe Down stream to supplement the main leat.

Beyond Lake Viaduct a large compost heap occupies the trackbed. From here return to Bridestowe Station; drive northward; turn right into Collaven Lane beyond Lake hamlet; park near the railway bridge. The view south is the deep cutting reaching to Lake Viaduct; north, the fence beyond the private stretch passing Collaven Cottage. Drive again northward; turn right into a lane marked 'To East Tor Farm'; park before reaching the railway bridge, but with discretion, as tractors use all gateways here. Ascend to the railway south of the bridge and walk to the Collaven Cottage fence, crossing (bridge intact) a sunken lane with grassy bed and twisting walls. Return northward and continue, with the tower of Bridestowe church directly ahead, across the East Tor bridge (intact). Here occurs another compost heap, but it is easily bypassed. A rock cutting follows, the compact rock having apparently needed much blasting. Hall Lane Bridge at Sourton is soon reached, beyond which the line passes along the east boundary of a new burial ground in Sourton churchyard; the typical Dartmoor tower, crocketed and embattled, of the lovely old church rises behind; the moor rushes upward on the east side and the whole scene breathes utter peace. Beyond the church the line is spanned by a private road-bridge before passing through a shallow cutting, followed by a low embankment across the foot of Sourton Down and Prewley Moor. The branch road to Prewley waterworks is bridged by the railway (span removed), leading to the open common of Prewley Moor, where the car should next be parked.

Walk northward. The up-gradient is appreciable, and the thrilling, spinning 80mph (129kph) run of the great expresses steaming down this stretch towards Lake Viaduct is easily imagined – though speed had to be reduced to 45mph (72kph) to cross the viaduct. Corn Ridge topped by Bronescombe's Loaf rises in the moorland background, the waterworks forming a less inspiring, though inoffensive feature in the near distance. Left of the works the land rises to the crest of Vellake Down, beyond which the fine peak of Yes Tor (2,030ft (619m)) presents a

122

remote, blue silhouette. The line passes behind houses near Sourton Cross (junction of the A30 and A386 roads) and enters the impressive curved Prewley Cutting, which carries it across Prewley Summit – at 950ft (289m) the highest point attained by the SR system. Mr Arthur Westlake of Okehampton, a retired BR area supervisor, remembers when the snowdrifts of 1962 filled the cutting to a depth of 20ft (6m); for one night and a day, he told me, a passenger train, two goods trains and two would-be rescue engines, were solidly trapped. The entire cutting was encased in ice in 1947 and 1952, when I saw the 'ammil' on north-west Dartmoor – an ice-coating on every tor visible from the SR line.

Prewley Cutting opens upon a short fenced-off level, which should be avoided. Return to the car, therefore, and drive to the final walking point. Beyond Sourton Cross, a by-road branches right from the A30 (here a wide, long descent) signposted 'Meldon'; take this, bear right in the hamlet, pass under the railway bridge and park. Enter upon the line through a roadside gateway. Walk southward to the farming enclosure near Prewley Cutting. Return, observing the now visible tips of Meldon Quarry and the high embankment approaching Meldon Junction, where another embankment converges on a huge curve and the scant remains of the platform lie where they meet – the foundations of the signalbox being up-line. Here, for some purpose, was a siding. Starting from the 'Bude Bay' at Okehampton Station, one could steam away under the towering, remote heights of West Mil Tor and Yes Tor into North Cornwall, until the Beeching Report resulted in the closure of the branch line in the summer of 1966 – a then unsuspected harbinger of the closure of the main line two years later. Continue northward from Meldon Junction beyond the parked car. The lane beneath the bridge (intact) is the King Way (see p81) descending from Vellake Gate. Beyond the bridge a 200yd (183m) stretch of embanked line brings the walker to the barrier-gate of Meldon Viaduct, where are large and unambiguous warnings against trespass. From here is seen the still remaining permanent way, commencing 60yd (55m) south of the viaduct,

Plate 17 A late-nineteenth-century view of Meldon Viaduct. Left to right: lime-works and access road to Meldon hamlet; the West Ockment River; leat to glass-works; narrow-gauge tramroad prefabricated in 12ft lengths to carry granulite in tip-trucks (visible at end of tramroad) from quarry behind camera point to works (horses provided motive power and stable still remains); gate on access road for horse-drawn cart delivery of glass bottles to Okehampton area; wooden steps for use of workmen to and from railway halt, with rails for manual haulage of light equipment in trucks (*The Francis Frith Collection*)

linking Meldon Quarry through Okehampton and Crediton with Exeter. Above the clanking sounds of conveyor machines and the grinding of stone-crushing plants there rises from time to time the shriek of a shunter and the low-pitched hooter of a powerful freight locomotive. Here the railway lives still, albeit no longer to serve the fare-paying passenger. The walk is finished.

Meldon is in an area of great geological complexity on the edge of the Dartmoor granite, that is, on the *metamorphic aureole*, and the previously existing country rock was violently affected by the molten magma intrusion of 290 million years ago. The tremendous metamorphosis that took place produced slates with lenticles, dolerite intrusions, aplite dykes, cherts, garnets, wollastonite and other fascinating mineral variations. Existing Upper Devonian slates became a dark, spotted rock known as 'hornfels', the substance now quarried and processed for use as permanent way ballast. About 400,000 tons are produced annually and despatched daily on trains of hopper wagons; the addition to this figure of sand and chippings brings the total to $\frac{1}{2}$ million tons, the ballast travelling throughout the Southern and Western Regions of BR as far as Reading and Bristol. The viaduct is in use now only as a 'shunting tail', providing additional space for that purpose.

The railway viaduct has six girder spans on metal lattice piers, the tallest 120ft (34.1m). Views moorward from its parapet, left to right, are of Black Down (Ockment), West Mil Tor, Longstone Hill, Homerton Hill and Corn Ridge topped by Bronescombe's Loaf; below is the reservoir, the old Meldon limestone and Redaven aplite quarries and the glassworks, the river and Meldon Pool. The vital maintenance of this metal

Plate 18 Engine-driver's view of Meldon Viaduct (photographed from a locomotive cab, June 1982). Meldon dam is left of centre, and beyond are Homerton Hill, Corn Ridge and Meldon Down

Plate 19 A stone train from Meldon Quarry entering Okehampton Station, June 1982. The total load is 1,007 tons. On the left is the 'Bude' bay

bridge, so surprisingly slender for its function in such an intemperate zone, seized the imagination of Eden Phillpotts, whose character 'Old Abner Barkell':

> ... passed the latter phase of his existence under the shadow of the mighty steel structure he had assisted to build ... He knew the bridge as a watchmaker knows a watch or an engineer his engine ... When the viaduct was being painted, men, looking no larger than spiders, hung from ropes about it. Mr Abner Barkell took a very live interest in these operations and buzzed hither and thither. The painters often wished him away ...

Seen from the river — its passage so noisy before the reservoir depleted it as to drown the sound of trains overhead — Phillpotts observed in *The Portreeve* that:

> Meldon Viaduct hung like a spider's web of silver above the mists of the gorge ... The iron way floated above, frail and delicate ... a thousand tons of steel supporting a thoroughfare whereon forty thousand human souls sped yearly across the dizzy depths below.

126

There are no restrictions on movement for those wishing to follow either river bank and view the viaduct from below.

British Rail have kindly enabled me to experience something of the past by riding on the footplate of *Implacable*, a type 50 diesel-electric locomotive hauling stone from Meldon Quarry. Arriving at Meldon, Driver A. W. May edged the powerful engine to the very girders of the viaduct (see Plate 18 on p125), prohibited from moving a foot nearer by the notice 'Open for shunters and empty wagons only', before reversing to couple to the stone train. With a train of 21 wagons weighing 1,007 tons – the average Inter-City train, in contrast, weighs about 350 tons – we drew gently away and threaded the lush vegetation of Okehampton Park, high above the river and the Norman castle, to approach Okehampton's ghost station. The long, capacious siding below the road overbridge (the Okehampton town–Battle Camp road), built for military use, is now rarely used. Still in place are the large hinged iron flaps once lowered to enable vehicles to be driven off the Surbiton car trains (see below). The LSWR opened their station at Okehampton, at an elevation of 750ft (227m), high above the town, in 1871. Its destiny, 101 years in passenger traffic, was better than that of many stations west of Exeter. Arthur Westlake (p123), who lives still in the terraced house overlooking the station where his daily work lay, is saddened to see its buildings neglected and decaying. When he was foreman on the Exeter and North Cornwall lines during the 1950s, his daily schedule on the Okehampton–Lydford line ran like this: 9 goods trains up: Exeter–Crediton–Okehampton–Lydford–Plymouth; 7 down; 7 stone trains from Meldon Quarry; 20 passenger trains, including the Brighton express and Atlantic Coast Express each way. Arthur, a man of ideas, is really the originator of 'Motorail'. In 1955 he suggested the running of the 'Surbiton Car Train' from London to Devon, with Okehampton as the western terminal. This was put into operation on summer Fridays and Saturdays and became well patronised.

14
GWR: Newton Abbot–Moretonhampstead Branch

12 miles (19.3km)   Map 14

Historical digest
Route surveyed 1848; construction delayed; opened 4 July 1866.
Absorbed by SDR 1872, latter by GWR 1876. Ascends from 25 to
550ft (8 to 168m); no tunnels or viaducts; pastoral country
railroad under Dartmoor's eastern edge, through woods and
meadows, accompanying Wray Brook (tributary of Bovey).
GWR introduced Moretonhampstead–Chagford bus service
1906. Passenger traffic grew with Torbay's popularity; road
competition significant after World War II; BR outmoded
timetable regrettably retained; passenger service withdrawn 2
March 1959, freight beyond Bovey Tracey 1964; 1971 special
'last' one-day passenger service, then rails lifted beyond
Heathfield and station demolished. BR freight service continues,
Newton Abbot–Heathfield light industries.

Following the line
Again the kindness of British Rail enables me to draw a complete
picture of a railroad still in partial use. Standing on the old
Moreton platform at Newton Abbot Station, I recalled often
changing here for an 'all-stations-to-Plymouth' train during my
early days of Dartmoor exploration. The platform is now the
Motorail terminal for the Stirling run.
　　Together with Inspector Harris and the locomotive crew, I
boarded a class 31/294 diesel at a 'through' platform and we
headed up-line to collect a clay train from Heathfield. Passing
the largest remaining manual signalbox on BR Western Region
and the former goods depot (now a leisure complex), we were
switched on to the branch line. This crosses the River Lemon and
the foot of the Whitelake Channel (tail of the old Stover Canal),
runs alongside the River Teign and under Kingsteignton road-

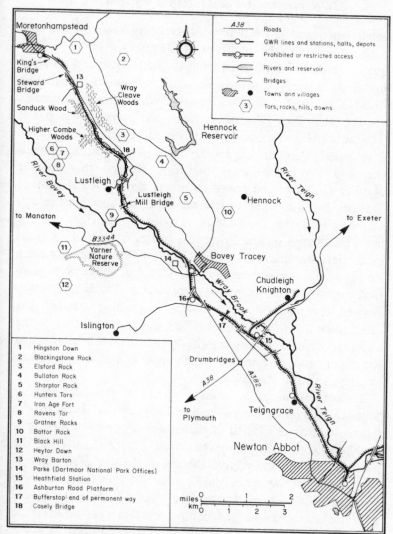

Moretonhampstead

King's Bridge

Steward Bridge

Sanduck Wood

Higher Combe Woods

River Bovey

to Manaton

Wray Cleave Woods

Hennock Reservoir

Lustleigh

Lustleigh Mill Bridge

B3344

Yarner Nature Reserve

River Teign

to Exeter

Hennock

Bovey Tracey

Chudleigh Knighton

Islington

Wray Brook

Drumbridges

A38

A382

to Plymouth

Teigngrace

River Teign

Newton Abbot

Heathfield Station

1 Hingston Down
2 Blackingstone Rock
3 Elsford Rock
4 Bullaton Rock
5 Sharptor Rock
6 Hunters Tors
7 Iron Age Fort
8 Ravens Tor
9 Gratner Rocks
10 Bottor Rock
11 Black Hill
12 Heytor Down
13 Wray Barton
14 Parke (Dartmoor National Park Offices)
15 Heathfield Station
16 Ashburton Road Platform
17 Bufferstop: end of permanent way
18 Casely Bridge

miles 0   1   2
km 0 1 2 3

Map 14 GWR Newton Abbot–Mortonhampstead branch

bridge. Passing a short clay siding and crossing the canal (which remains close beside the railway to its terminal basin), we reached Teignbridge level crossing. North of this, industry is left behind and the sights and sounds of the countryside are uninhibited, the track speed limit of 15mph (24kph) certainly assisting rural observation. At Teigngrace the line passes a canal basin and old buildings where barges were built and, a short way on, the platform of Teigngrace Halt. On this quiet stretch of line, hidden from the casual eye and set amid meadows, waterfowl, gamebirds, foxes, willows and crumbling canal locks, the Royal Train is parked when a royal personage, visiting the West Country, needs an overnight stop. At Teigngrace Halt is a siding with clay-loading ramp, now disused. Two underbridges carrying country lanes soon follow, and a third the A38 Plymouth–Exeter highway. Beyond this are the platforms, sidings and remnants of the demolished Heathfield Station; the junction of the truncated Teign Valley line through Christow to Exeter (St Thomas) is passed on the right, and the last underbridge on the living line brings it to the Heathfield industrial establishments where the Gulf Oil Company have a siding; here, once or twice a week, a train of about twenty-two tank wagons, the oil company's own, carries oil to their terminal. Beyond the junction of main line and siding appears that unwelcome sign of contemporary railroad economic distress, the terminal buffer-stop; easing right up to it, Driver Nation halted the engine and we removed to the opposite end for the return journey with the clay load.

To readers about to embark upon the practical task of following the remainder of the line, I suggest they disregard the length immediately north of the buffer-stop; in any case, one could reach it only from the south by trespassing on the permanent way, while from the north the site of the line is swallowed by industrial development. Drive, therefore, to Granite Siding, Bovey Tracey (see Map 10). Walk southward until the line vanishes in pits, hollows and factory enclosures (the walk enhanced by a wild magnolia tree on the trackbed) observing the lonely, clay-based heathland through which it passes. Return; continue northward from Granite Siding, passing below Pottery Bridge and behind the Bovey Pottery. The line remains clear for some way behind a housing development, until the overgrown platform of a halt brings it to Ashburton Road Bridge in Bovey Tracey. The underside of the bridge is blocked with earth, stones and brambles; therefore ascend a path

Plate 20 Engine-driver's view of Teignbridge Crossing (photographed from a locomotive cab, June 1982), with the crossing-keeper's cottage on the right. On the left is the Watts, Blake & Bearne clay-loading ramp

(right) to the road and pass over/through the roadside fences and descend to the line beyond the bridge, where rough steps have been cut in the bank. Beyond the crossing of a footpath and stream the buildings of Bovey Tracey Station come in sight, a view so reminiscent of the approach to a country station from the window of a branch-line 'stopper'. Nearer the station gardens encroach upon the line, so turn left into a lineside road (Blenheim Terrace): on reaching Widecombe Road, turn right, then left into the station yard. If a close-up view of buildings and platforms is desired, apply to the Dartmoor National Park Authority (the present owners) at nearby Parke. The original canopy and engine shed remain, both platforms are intact and the goods siding is accessible. Bordering the station yard are the premises of millers and seedsmen Wyatt & Bruce. This, once the largest flour mill in the district, was served by a rail siding. At the up-line end of the yard a barrier gate and fence have been erected across the line.

Next, drive towards the town centre and turn right before reaching the river (Bovey) bridge, into the (free) car park. From here set out to walk along the line to Lustleigh. Cross the road and follow the river (south bank) through New Park, a delightful place where the Men of the Trees have planted about two hundred trees and placed rustic tables and benches. The further boundary of the park is provided by the low railway embankment; from here notice the various details of nearby Bovey Station beyond the barrier gate. Continue northward. The placid River Bovey (bridge intact) heralds the beginning of a beautiful woodland glade, where the line crosses a deeply sunken lane between the estates of Parke and Southbrook and passes a plate-layers' hut of the modern concrete type. Walking here calls for strong footwear as sharp ballast continues for some distance uncovered by grass. A level crossing leads into the Parke woodlands and an underbridge carries a stony track ascending from a ford on the river. To gain relief from ballast-walking and to appreciate the lovely surroundings of the railroad, ascend to the bridge and emerge into an open field enclosed by woodlands, to where comes a fine view (west) of Black Hill 1,000ft (305m) above (see Map 10), and bear left to a stile; follow the undulating path beyond, which ascends to skirt the edge of another field before again diving into the woods. The path reaches a steep lane; here return downhill to the line at a rail overbridge (span removed) near a junction of lanes. The northward lane leads to Knowle, beyond which Hawkmoor Sanatorium appears in its wooded setting on the east valley side, and the up-line walker has his first meeting with Wray Brook; this passes under the lane and through a conduit with granite portals beneath the railroad to join the River Bovey beside the westward lane, which crosses the river in the midst of this beautiful glade of three bridges. Between river and railway runs a third lane, to Lustleigh, all three tight together. A hillside cutting brings the line to another bridge (intact), north of which a platform has at some time been built of sleepers and is approached via stile and gate on a footpath from Lower Hisley. The next bridge (intact) is a fine, double-arch structure over a lane to Manaton; next comes a farm level crossing, a hillside cutting and a high-level bridge (of three arches over the winding Wray Brook). This stretch of line – from

Knowle Lane via a broken bridge at Rudge Lane and a lineside piggery to Lustleigh Mill Bridge where the line crosses a swift stream almost at viaduct height (double-arch bridge, intact), so deep-hidden in the heart of the countryside – is very satisfying.

From Lustleigh Mill Bridge progress is more troublesome and a thicket of brambles means lacerated bare knees. As the line clears it approaches a fence near the first houses of Lustleigh village; a private garden follows, so return down-line and drive to Lustleigh Station, now the private residence of Mr Mike Jacobs, who asks that intending visitors should write to him at The Old Railway Station, Lustleigh, Newton Abbot, Devon, TQ13 9PL, for permission to walk along the platform (intact) down-line, past the coal siding and yard, to a broken bridge; on the right are the roofs, ancient and modern, of the village (including the Cleave Hotel, nearest the line) and the church tower, and on the left the pleasant, emerald green spread of the recreation ground. The flower gardens at old Lustleigh Station, tended by the stationmaster, were celebrated, and to this day roses assert themselves colourfully among the buildings. From the bridge abutment is visible the fence north of Lustleigh Mill Bridge, the intervening embankment (private property) having been partly excavated.

Obstacles to following the railroad literally – beginning at the fence mentioned – continue for some distance up-line. The trackbed is impenetrably overgrown even before the station underbridge is reached and continues so through Casely Cutting to Casely Bridge (intact). One may mount to the bridge and walk up-line for a few hundred yards, only to be halted by another jungle which, with intermediate clearings not accessible to the public, extends to a point in Higher Combe Wood opposite East Wray. North of the wood the line is relatively unimpeded to Moretonhampstead, excepting a stretch between Wray Barton and Steward Bridge. To follow it, make the approach at Wray Barton, first calling at 'Hartlands' (west side of lane overbridge) to ask permission from Mr and Mrs L. G. Pearse to follow and park a car. The bridge contains an integral lane on one side of the roadway through which farm animals passed from field to farmyard without straying on to the road. Permission obtained, enter the roadside gate (east end of bridge) and descend to the line. A good clear stretch runs southward below the lumpy little hills under Dartmoor's edge, made the more pleasant by the accompanying Wray Brook; a broken bridge causes no problem; simply pass through a gate (left) and rejoin the line beyond; nearby is an ancient bridge carrying the valley road over the brook. Higher Combe Wood, where Fountain Forestry operate, is entered at a wide gate and walking remains easy to a point opposite East Wray, a one-time farm at the brookside. (Use discretion, however, as the trackbed is not a public right of way.) The line, overgrown but passable, enters East Wray Cleave and the sound of a waterfall grows near. Wray Brook passes through the Cleave (here a miniature gorge) and is inviting to ear and eye on a hot day, but further progress is impossible, for this marks the northern extent of the overgrown stretch encountered above Casely Bridge.

Return to Wray Barton, the white gables of the house reflecting sunlight against the cool green shades of Wray Cleave Woods; continue up-line. The railroad is visible from the road north of Wray Barton with one or two intermediate open stretches; walkers should not, however, cross farm fields to reach them for they are unremarkable and the delightful topography of the line between Wray Barton and East Wray may be taken as typical of the remainder. My abiding memory of travelling this line is of the woodlands – Higher Combe and Sanduck Woods in particular – where smoke- and steam-wreathed tree-tops on the ascending trip as the engine tackled the gradient and granite outcrops began to appear high on the east valley side near Blackingstone Rock.

The overgrown line finally clears at Steward Bridge (span removed), where the huge Steward Farm lies west of the road, and Steward Mill, east. Continue driving past the settlement and turn right into a lane signposted 'Budleigh Farm' (marked on maps as 'Budleigh'); here ask permission to follow the line in each direction and park a car. The line formerly crossed Budleigh Lane on a bridge and embankment, both since removed. Enter a gateway to walk southward. Passing behind Steward Mill (now a private residence), notice the ornamental millpond and large waterwheel. Just ahead is the abutment of Steward Bridge, where one may contemplate the scene as traffic passes below on the Moretonhampstead–Newton Abbot road. Return, with the tower of Moretonhampstead church now in sight; cross Budleigh Lane and an open field to reach King's Bridge (span removed); the last lap is in sight, Moretonhampstead goods shed appearing $\frac{1}{4}$ mile (0.4km) ahead. Return to the car and drive to the station, now the premises of Messrs B. Thompson & Sons (Transport) Ltd. Happily, the firm's Managing Director, Mr R. H. Thompson, is in sympathy with railway preservation. Thompsons became the overall owners of the site only after a previous firm occupying the north end of the station had indiscriminatingly demolished the water tower and station offices. Mr Thompson is proud to show visitors the intact platform and the goods shed still in use as such. Through a huge arch in the east wall carts and lorries once entered to load goods brought up by train; Thompsons' vehicles now use a south entrance to the shed, the indoor trackbed having been concreted. The engine shed, too, in good condition, still shelters maintenance workers – now servicing internal combustion engines and articulated trailer mechanisms. Beyond the engine shed (and lorry yard) an avenue of bushes indicates the old line to Newton Abbot. Follow it to the north abutment of King's Bridge. Returning, notice how predominant is the tower of Moretonhampstead parish church above the roofs of the ancient town. Reaching the station, pass (for realism's sake) along the platform and around Thompsons' offices (built by their predecessors on the site of the demolished station building); on leaving the yard observe the original GWR gates and iron posts; these, Mr Thompson told me, are due for restoration. This railroad-conscious Managing Director asks that visitors call at the office on arrival.

15
GWR: Buckfastleigh–Ashburton

2½ miles (4km)   Map 1

A vanished railroad

Regretfully, this reputedly delightful, rural link with the main GWR line at Totnes cannot be followed for it was entirely obliterated, except at the upper terminus, in the construction of the A38 dual carriageway in 1974. I also regret having no personal memories of the line, one which I had no occasion to use. Opened on 1 May 1872 by the SDR Company, it formed the railhead of the beautiful Dart Valley branch line, now very much alive between Totnes and Buckfastleigh as a 'preserved' steam-traction railway (and described in the author's *Historic Dart*), successfully operated by the Dart Valley Railway Association since 1969.

Leaving Buckfastleigh Station the line crossed the River Dart over a girder bridge on stone piers, later demolished to make way for the new A38 bridge, and at each end of which were signals. It then followed the east bank of the River Ashburn (where the original hillside cutting remained to serve the new road) to pass Pridhamsleigh Barton, Cave and Quarry; the latter, now disused, was then worked by Hoare Bros, and a quarry official had to attend at Buckfastleigh Station daily before blasting took place (9.45–10.15am) in order to enquire whether any train stood on the Ashburton line; if so, blasting had to be delayed. Beyond the quarry, the line passed through the lower fields of Pridhamsleigh Barton, its route now quite vanished beneath the highway. With the eastward curve of this at the foot of Yolland Hill, it left the riverside meadow opposite the Pear Tree Garage and occupied a cutting (now in-filled for the passage of the A38 sliproad) densely overgrown between these two points. Two very

136

large boulders of metamorphic rock lie near the roadside, where a footpath runs above the west side of the cutting. This leads to the point where the Old Totnes Road crossed the line to enter the town, beyond which the cutting remains in its original state and, being occupied by a public footpath ('Bulliver's Way') is kept free from overgrowth. The old railway fences remain in places and the path leads to Whistley Bridge, where Chuley Road descends from Whistley Hill to enter the town. River, railway and highway sharply delineate the town boundary here, for not a single building appears beyond them to the east. Beside Chuley Road, the line emerges from the cutting and approaches Ashburton Station, where GWR chocolate-and-cream is still in evidence. The original overall wooden roof now shelters the Station Garage of Mr W. F. Wills; here, with permission, it is possible to see the three arched entrances (from the former west platform) to the lamp room, ticket office and waiting-room. The cattle siding and pen, once in regular use, stood at the east side of the station. The spacious station entrance was approached from St Lawrence Lane, the engine shed is now a grain store, and the goods shed still retains its wooden canopy over the goods siding. It happened that the lie of the land made it possible to site the station nearer the town centre than was usually the case in Devon's hilly towns.

The considerable amount of freight, including ore from the Dart Valley mines, carried on the branch helped in later years to compensate for falling passenger receipts. Coal and farm fertiliser were brought in, and outgoing commodities included umber (locally mined), malt, milk, and rabbits from Huntingdon Warren on southern Dartmoor. As with the lower portion of the line between Buckfastleigh and Totnes, the rails were left in place – at least until being lifted to make way for the new highway. All traffic on the line ceased in October 1971, and on the final day of operation, according to Frank Booker in *The History of the GWR*, through trains were run to Ashburton from London and South Wales.

Epilogue

It is a truism that we do not cherish a possession until it is lost, and now we might well reproach ourselves for not having spent more leisure time – for what only then was a small outlay – in travelling over our unique country railroads when they were still there to use. An account of many such lines is given in David St John Thomas' *The Country Railway*. Such a heading should remind the present reader, too, that in following the Dartmoor railroads he is lamenting the passing of both branch lines and such main rail arteries as the outstanding SR line from Exeter to Plymouth via Okehampton, Lydford and Tavistock (North). On 6 May 1968, that last nebulous thread of steam and smoke was borne by Dartmoor's prevailing wind back across the viaduct to Meldon – which 'hung like a spider's web above the mists of the gorge' – steam, smoke and mist blending into one immense cloud such as so often veils the age-old tors above. Some 1,200ft (366m) below them, that little, ephemeral plaything of man, the train on its Dartmoor railroad, had disturbed the silence of the granite peaks for the last time.

Acknowledgements

The author wishes to express his gratitude to the undermentioned persons for their co-operation, assistance and courtesy:

K. E. Allerfield; Maurice Anning; Cliff Bagg; D. H. Baker, British Rail; Eric Blachford, DNP; H. W. Castleton; Paul Chapman; I. J. Coon; J. Curtis; A. S. Dumpleton, British Rail; H. R. Duncan, HM Prison, Princetown; Commander David Ellingham, RN retd, CEng, MIEE; E. W. T. Flemington, Western Machinery; Mrs G. F. Garbutt; The Deputy Governor, HM Prison, Princetown; Mike Harman, Fairey Winches Ltd; Inspector R. J. Harris, British Rail; W. E. Harvey & Son; George Heesem; John Howe; D. M. Hutton; Mike Jacobs; Brian Johnson, Johnson & Baxter Ltd; Mrs Jill Johnson; Graham Jones; Philip Jones, ECLP Ltd; Mrs J. Lake; Brian Lavis; William Lavis; Philip Lee, ECLP Ltd; Commander C. O. Lombi; A. W. May, British Rail; Gordon May, ECLP Ltd; Mr & Mrs G. Medland; Mrs M. A. Mudge; I. Nation, British Rail; H. S. Nicholson; G. Osborne, British Rail; Mr and Mrs L. G. Pearse; A. J. Pellow; Frank G. Quant; Paul Rawlings, Tecalemit Ltd; Arthur Read; John Savery snr; T. J. Skelton, ECLP Ltd; Bert Spencer, Amey Roadstone Corporation; Colonel C. R. Spencer; J. F. H. Stabb; M. Stephens-Hodge; Mrs J. Sterne; Miss C. Symons; R. H. Thompson; Hedley Walters; Mr and Mrs L. R. Watson; Watts, Blake & Bearne Ltd; Inspector S. E. Webb, British Rail; West Devon Borough Council; A. G. Westlake; W. F. Wills; Mrs A. R. Wilson and staff of the Local History Department, Plymouth City Library.

The author's son, Gabriel Hemery, was of particular assistance during field-work.

Bibliography

Anthony, G. H. *The Tavistock, Launceston & Princetown Railway* (Oakwood Press, 1979)

Ewans, M. C. *The Haytor Granite Tramway and Stover Canal* (David & Charles, 1977)

Fairclough and Shepherd. *Mineral Railways of the West Country* (Bradford Barton, 1975)

Fairclough and Wills. *More Southern Steam in the West Country* (Bradford Barton, 1975)

——*Southern Steam in the West Country* (Bradford Barton, 1973)

Gill, Crispin (ed). *Dartmoor: A New Study* (David & Charles, 1970)

——*Plymouth, A New History* (David & Charles, 1979)

Hall, R. M. S. *Lee Moor Tramway* (Oakwood Press (undated))

Harris, Helen. *Industrial Archaeology of Dartmoor* (David & Charles, 1972)

Hemery, Eric. *High Dartmoor – Land and People* (Robert Hale, 1983)

—— *Historic Dart* (David & Charles, 1982)

Hoskins, W. G. *Devon* (David & Charles, 1982)

Kendall, H. G. *Plymouth & Dartmoor Railway* (Oakwood Press, 1968)

Kingdom, A. R. *The Ashburton Branch* (Oxford Publishing Company, 1976)

Morley Estate Papers. (West Devon Record Office, Plymouth)

Nash, Sydney. *Southern Region Steam Album* (Ian Allan, 1967)

Railway plans, various original. (Devon Record Office, Exeter)

Roche, T. W. E. *The Withered Arm* (Forge Books, 1967)

Rolt, L. T. C. *The Potters' Field* (David & Charles, 1974)

Stabb I. and Downing, T. *The Redlake Tramway and the China Clay Industry* (privately printed)

St John Thomas, D. *The Country Railway* (David & Charles, 1976)

—— *A Regional History of the Railways of Great Britain:* Vol 1, *The West Country* (David & Charles, 1981)

Index